TRIUMPH

OWNER'S HANDBOOK

Publication Part No. 545111/73

Issued by
TRIUMPH MOTORS
BRITISH LEYLAND U.K. LTD.
COVENTRY, ENGLAND

A member of the British Leyland Motor Corporation

TRIUMPH TR6

Introduction

DESIGNED AND BUILT *to give long and consistent trouble-free service, your TR6 embodies many new safety features, the very presence of which will add to your confidence.*

Read carefully the contents of this book which gives, in the simplest possible terms, information vital to the proper operation, care and regular maintenance of the car.

The TR6 complies with, and in many cases exceeds, all current Federal and State Regulations concerning Safety, Engine Crankcase Emission and Fuel Evaporative Control.

Because of these regulations, owners are strongly urged to make use of the Passport to Service and to read the Emission Control System, Maintenance and Warranty information in this handbook. The operations carried out by your Distributor or Dealer will be in accordance with the current recommendations and may be subject to revision from time to time.

These publications should be passed to each subsequent owner of the vehicle and the Servicing Details completed to ensure that the vehicle is kept within the Federal limits in respect of the Clean Air Acts.

Important

In all communications relating
to Service or Spares, please quote
the Commission Number
(Chassis Number)
Paint and Trim Numbers

LOCATION OF COMMISSION AND UNIT NUMBERS

Note. L.H. and R.H. refer to Left-hand and Right-hand side of the vehicle viewed from the driving position.

Commission, Paint and Trim Numbers—On rear door pillar (may be seen by opening driver's door). Also on a tag visible through the windscreen on the left hand windscreen pillar.

Engine Number—On L.H. side of Cylinder Block

Gearbox Number—On L.H. side of Housing

Rear Axle Number—On Hypoid Housing Flange

STANPART

Spare Parts Service

Replacement parts are not supplied from the factory direct to the general public, but are directed through Distributors who, in turn, supply their Dealers.

Genuine spare parts are marketed under the trade mark "Stanpart" and carry the same guarantee as the original part. The same high quality material is used and the strictest accuracy maintained during manufacture. You are advised, therefore, to insist on the use of these parts should replacements be necessary. Remember, parts which do not carry the trade mark "Stanpart" will invalidate the guarantee if fitted to your vehicle.

The descriptions and illurtrations appearing in this book are not binding. The MANUFACTURER, therefore, reserves the right — whilst retaining the basic features of the Models herein described and illustrated — to make at any time, without necessarily bringing this book up-to-date, any alteration to units, parts or accessories deemed convenient for improvement or for any manufacturing or commercial reason.

List of Sections

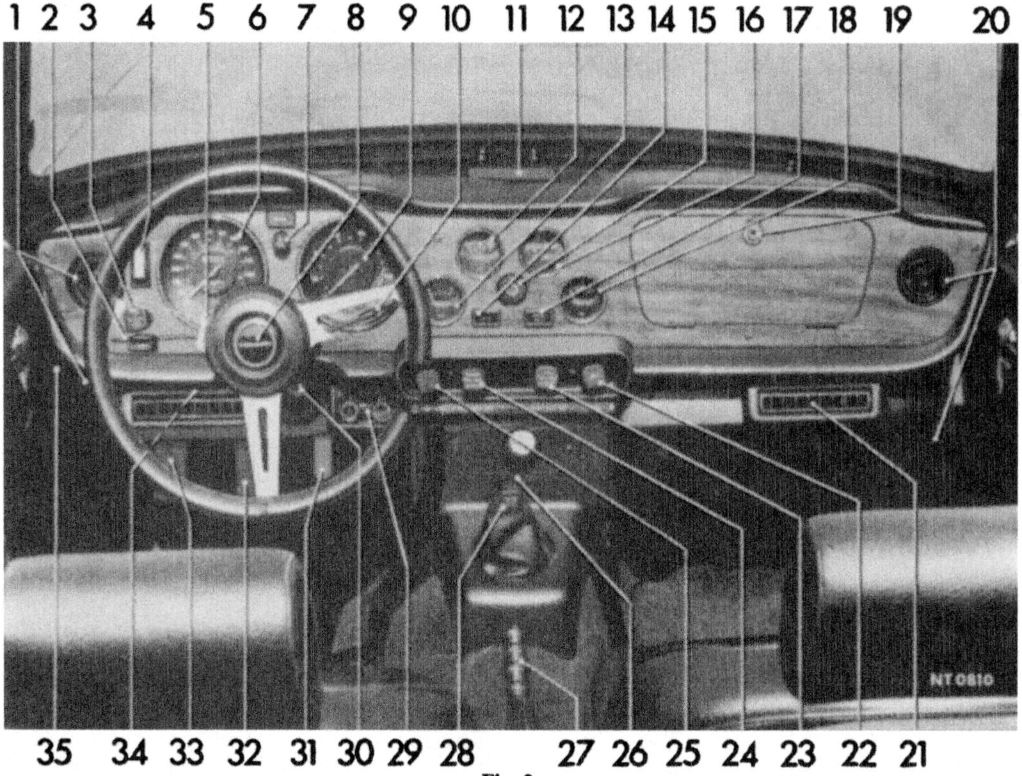

1 2 3 4 5 6 7 8 9 10 11 12 13 14 15 16 17 18 19 20

35 34 33 32 31 30 29 28 27 26 25 24 23 22 21

Fig. 2

KEY TO FIG. 2

1. Fresh-air vents
2. Turn-signal control
3. Windshield wiper washer switch
4. Lighting switch
5. Overdrive switch (optional)
6. Speedometer
7. Hazard warning switch and indicator
8. Horn-push
9. Tachometer
10. Headlight dipper switch
11. Ashtray
12. Oil pressure gauge
13. Temperature gauge
14. Brake-line failure indicator
15. Instrument illumination rheostat
16. Fuel gauge
17. Seat belt warning indicator
18. Voltmeter
19. Glove-box lock
20. Fresh-air vents
21. Air conditioning (optional) outlets
22. Choke control
23. Heat control
24. Blower switch
25. Air distribution control
26. Gear shift lever
27. Parking-brake lever
28. Interior light switch
29. Air conditioning (optional) control panel
30. Ignition/steering column lock
31. Throttle pedal
32. Brake pedal
33. Clutch pedal
34. Trip zero control
35. Bonnet release control
36. High-beam indicator
37. Turn-signal indicator
38. Low oil pressure indicator
39. No-charge indicator
40. Odometer
41. Trip odometer

Refer to Fig. 5

CONTROLS, INSTRUMENTS AND INDICATORS

The controls, instruments and indicators shown on Figs. 2 and 6 and described in the following pages are positioned within easy reach of the driver to afford maximum ease of operation and minimum distraction. The bracketed figures in the text cross-refer with the key on page 7.

Fresh-Air Vents (1)

The swivelling vents can be adjusted to admit cold air only in any chosen direction within the limits of movement. Each vent incorporates a valve, operated by a knob in the center of the vent. To diminish or shut off the supply of air, turn the knob clockwise. The air flow may be boosted by use of the blower motor (See item 24).

Turn Signal Control (2)

Move the control lever upwards to operate the right-hand turn-signal lights or downwards to operate the left-hand turn-signal lights. See (37) Page 13.

Windshield Wiper Washer Switch

Depress the switch to spray clean fluid onto the windshield and release the switch when sufficient fluid has been dispensed.

Turn the switch clockwise to operate the wipers at slow speed and turn the switch clockwise again to operate the wipers at high speed. Turn the switch fully anticlockwise to switch the wipers off, when they will automatically return to the parked position at the base of the windshield.

The wipers and washer will only operate when the ignition switch is turned 'ON'.

Lighting Switch (4)

Depress the lower portion of the switch to the first position to illuminate the rear tail, license plate, parking lights and side marker lights.

Depress the switch again to the second position to illuminate the headlights. (See "Headlight Dipper", 10).

Overdrive Switch (5) (Optional)

When an overdrive unit is fitted to the vehicle the operating switch is mounted on the left-hand side of the steering column. Move the lever up to engage the overdrive and down to release it. Before using the control, refer to page 38.

Speedometer (6)

Additional to indicating the road speed of the vehicle in miles and kilometres per hour, the instrument also combines the turn signal and high beam warning lights and the total and trip odometers.

Hazard Warning Switch and Indicator (7)

If the vehicle is immobilised and constitutes a hazard to other vehicles, warning may be given by using the "hazard warning system". To operate, pull the switch (7) when all turn-signal lights will flash intermittently.

When the hazard switch is operated, a bulb in the switch will flash in unison with the exterior warning lamps.

Horn Push (8)

Press to operate the horns.

Tachometer (9)

The tachometer indicates the engine speed in revolutions per minute and combines two warning indicators (38, 39. See Fig. 5). The speed range within the colored segments is subject to the "Recommended Speed Limits" mentioned on page 38.

Headlight Dipper Switch (10)

When the headlights are illuminated (see 'Lighting Switch' on page 8), the high beams may be lowered by moving the lever down. To return to the high beam position, move the lever up.

The high beam position is indicated by a blue warning light (36) near the bottom of the speedometer dial.

Lifting the lever towards the steering wheel flashes the headlight high beams.

Ashtray (11)

An ashtray is provided in the center of the facia top. To empty, lift the assembly from the surround.

Oil Pressure Gauge (12)

Oil pressure at 2,000 r.p.m. under normal operating conditions, should be 45–65 lbs./sq. in. Severe operating conditions, such as competition work, may cause the oil pressure to drop below 25 lb./sq. in., indicating that the oil temperature is excessive. Under these circumstances fitment of an oil cooler may be necessary.

Temperature Gauge (13)

When the ignition switch is turned 'ON' the pointer moves slowly across the dial taking up to one minute to reach a true reading.

Normal operating temperature is reached when the pointer registers in the central sector of the dial. Should the pointer reach the highest mark, stop the engine immediately and check the level of coolant in the radiator. Refer to page 50.

Brake-line Failure Indicator (14)

When the ignition switch is turned on the "brake line failure" and "low oil pressure" indicator lights glow faintly and are extinguished when the engine is running. Should the failure of the front or rear brake lines occur, the indicator (14) will glow brightly.

A broken bulb filament is indicated by the warning light failing to glow when the ignition is turned on, before starting the engine.

Instrument Illumination Rheostat (15)

Turn the knob clockwise to illuminate the instruments. Further rotation of the knob diminishes the light intensity—operates only when the lighting switch is 'ON'.

Fuel Gauge (16)

The fuel gauge indicates the approximate contents of the fuel tank. When the ignition switch is turned 'ON' the pointer moves slowly across the dial taking up to one minute to reach a steady reading which it will maintain regardless of vehicle movement, until the ignition is switched 'OFF'.

Seat Belt Warning Indicator (17)

On models fitted with a seat belt warning device this lamp lights on the facia and a buzzer sounds if an attempt is made to drive the car without the seat belts in use.

Voltmeter (18)

This gauge is a battery condition indicator and registers the battery's state of charge. With the engine running above idling speed the indicator should register approximately 14 volts. A reading above 15 volts, which continues after 10 minutes running, is too high and should be investigated. A reading of 13 to 13·5 volts is too low unless the headlamps and other electrical equipment are in use.

Glove Box Lock (19)

The glove box may be unlocked by turning the key a quarter turn clockwise and opened by depressing the locking barrel.

Fresh Air Vents (20)

See (1) page 8.

Air Conditioning Outlet (21)

This is an optional item and reference should be made to the manufacturer's literature when it is fitted.

Choke Control (22)

This control is used to enrich the fuel mixture for easy starting from cold. The control should not be used if the engine is warm, and may not be necessary in warm climates. Full instructions for use are given on page 37.

Heat Control (23)

The heat control operates a water valve which regulates the flow of water through the heater unit. The control may be set at any intermediate position as required. The water valve is closed when the control is pushed in; maximum heat is available when the control is pulled out.

Blower Switch (24)

The blower motor boosts the flow of air through the heater unit. Pull the switch to its first position to operate the blower motor at slow speed or to its second position for high speed operation. The blower will operate only when the ignition switch is turned 'ON'.

Air Distribution Control (25)

The air distribution control operates a 'flap' valve which directs air from the heater unit to the windshield or to the windshield and interior. The maximum volume of air is directed to the windshield (for de-misting and de-frosting) when the control is pulled halfway out. When the control is pulled fully out, air is distributed to the interior and to the windshield. The 'flap' valve is closed when the control is pushed fully in.

Gear Shift Lever (26)

Moving the gear shift lever from neutral, the gear positions are as follows:

1st	.. ..	Move the lever left and forward
2nd	.. ..	Move the lever left and rearward
3rd	.. ..	Move the lever right and forward
4th (top)	..	Move the lever right and rearward
Reverse	..	Move the lever sharply to the extreme right and rearward. Engage only when the vehicle is stationary.

Always select neutral before starting the engine.

Parking Brake Lever (27)

To apply the rear wheel brakes pull the parking brake lever upwards. To release the brakes, pull the lever slightly upwards, depress the button (arrowed, Fig. 3) and lower the lever while the button is depressed.

Interior Light Switch (28)

The interior lamp is illuminated when the switch is pulled outwards.

The lamp is also automatically illuminated when either door is opened.

Air Conditioning Control Panel (29)

This is an optional item and reference should be made to the manufacturer's literature when it is fitted.

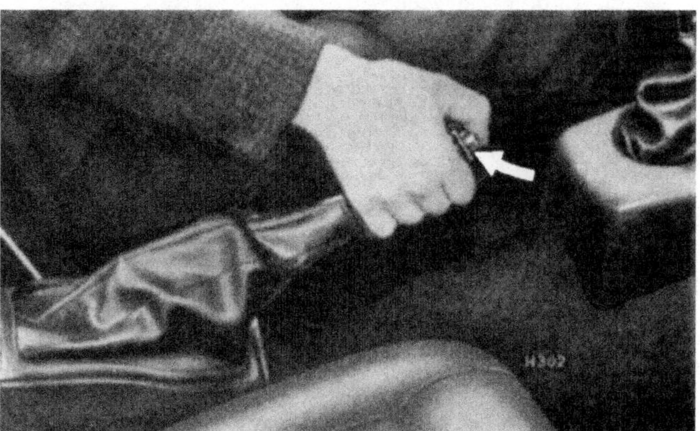

Fig. 3

Ignition, Starter and Steering Lock Switch (30)

The combined ignition/starter/steering lock switch is operated by a special key.

Incorporated in the switch is a "Key Warning System". The alarm system is fitted to encourage the driver to remove the ignition key from the lock before leaving the vehicle.

Separate keys are supplied for locking the driver's door. The switch has four positions (Fig. 4) as follows:

0   "OFF" in which position the key may be inserted or withdrawn (see Key Warning System, page 36).

I   "Auxiliary", in this position the ignition circuit is isolated to allow the use of a radio when the vehicle is stationary and the ignition is switched off.

II   "Ignition".

III   "Start" (Refer to "Starting the engine" on page 37).

Turn the key clockwise to II (Ignition) the ignition will be switched on.

To start the engine, the key should be turned a little more against spring pressure to III ("start"), as soon as the engine fires release the key which will return automatically under spring pressure to the ignition position (II).

1. To stop engine and engage steering lock

Turn the key in an anti-clockwise direction from the "ignition" position (II) to the "lock" position (0). This action stops the engine.

Removal of the key in this position automatically actuates the steering lock mechanism. (See Key Warning System. page 36).

If difficulty is experienced in removing the key, this can be rectified by simultaneous movement of the steering wheel.

The Key Warning System only functions when the ignition key is positioned in the switch and the driver's door is open. The "warning" denoted by a continuous buzzing sound will terminate when the driver's door is closed or the ignition key is completely removed. (See page 36).

2. To disengage Steering Lock and Start Engine

Insert the key and turn in clockwise direction. If difficulty is experienced in turning the key, this can be rectified by simultaneous movement of the steering wheel.

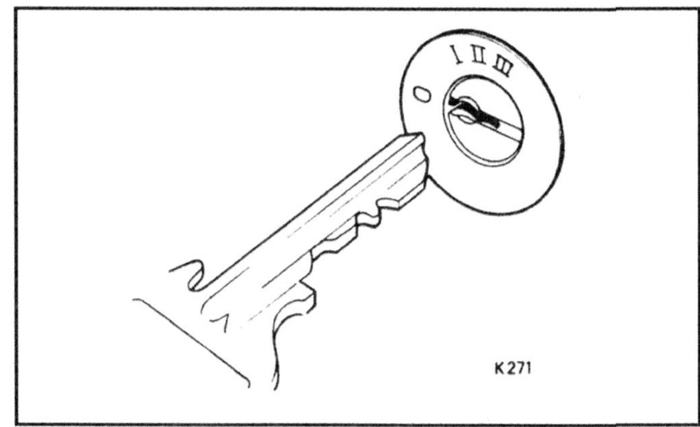

Fig. 4

Throttle, Brake and Clutch Pedals (31, 32 and 33)

These are conventional items which should require no further explanation.

Trip Zero Control (34)

The trip odometer (41) may be reset to zero by pushing the knob (34) upwards and turning anticlockwise.

Bonnet Release Control (35)

To open the bonnet, pull the control knob located below the parcel shelf at the left hand side of the car. This disengages the locking plate and allows the bonnet to rise sufficiently for the safety catch to be released using the fingers. See page 17.

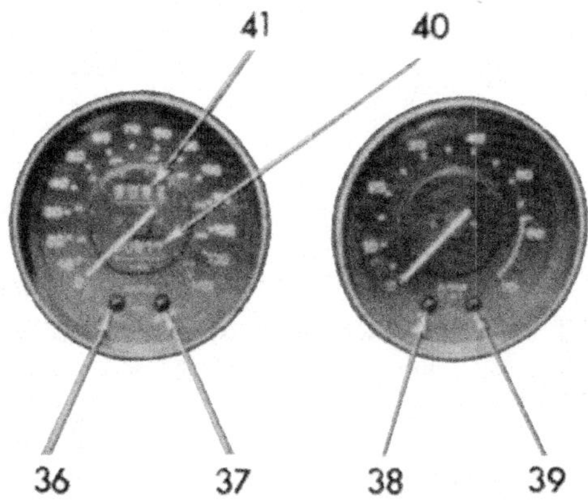

Fig. 5

High Beam Indicator (36, Fig. 5)

The indicator glows blue when the headlight high beams are selected and is extinguished when the headlights are 'dipped'.

Turn Signal Indicator (37, Fig. 5)

Indicates the correct functioning of the turn signal lights when operated by the lever (2). A broken filament in a bulb on one side of the vehicle is denoted by the non-operation of the indicator light when the lever is in the relevant operating position. A defective flasher unit or broken filament in the indicator bulb will be indicated by no light response from the lever in both directional positions.

Low Oil Pressure Indicator (38, Fig. 5)

The center indicator glows green when the ignition is switched on and is extinguished when the engine runs in excess of idling speed. Should the light remain on at normal running speeds, stop the engine and check the level of oil in the engine oil pan. If this is satisfactory, have the lubrication system checked immediately.

No-Charge Indicator (39, Fig. 5)

The indicator glows red when the ignition is switched on and is extinguished when the engine is running. Should the red light remain on whilst driving, a fault is indicated in the battery charging system which should be rectified without delay.

Odometer (40, Fig. 5)

The figures within the aperture below the center of the speedometer dial show the total mileage of the vehicle and may be used as a guide for periodic lubrication and maintenance.

Trip Odometer (41, Fig. 5)

The figures within the aperture above the center of the speedometer dial may be used to record the distance of each journey, provided that the figures are initially set at zero. (See 'Trip Zero Control', 34.)

Radio Controls

For operating instructions see the radio leaflet provided with the set.

Sun Visors

Two adjustable sun visors, padded to reduce the risk of impact injury, may be unclipped from the centre support brackets and swung to eliminate side glare. The passenger's sun viser incorporates a vanity mirror.

Rear View Mirror

The anti-glare device incorporated in the rear view mirror is operated by moving downwards the lever located on the rear of the mirror.

SAFETY HARNESS

Safety harness anchorage points are built into the vehicle and automatic, reel type safety belts are fitted before the car is delivered.

Using the Harness

Ensure that the buckle unit is conveniently situated by the side of the seat and pass the seat buckle over the shoulder nearest to the car door. With the lap and body belts passing across the body, plug the belt buckle into the nearest centre buckle unit. This is denoted by a positive 'click'.

To release the harness depress the marked panel on the centre buckle unit.

Note: The seat belt warning device will operate if an attempt is made to drive the car without the seat belts in use.

Cleaning

Badly stained safety belts can be dry cleaned. The cleaner should be advised of the nature of staining. Belts subjected to normal soiling can be cleaned with soap, or detergents dissolved in hot water.

Inertia Reel Mechanism Check

Every 10,000 km (6000 miles), carry out the following road check to ensure that the safety harness inertia reel mechanisms for both driver and passenger continue to operate satisfactorily.

IMPORTANT. Road tests must only be carried out under maximum safe road conditions, i.e. level, dry road with no following or oncoming traffic of any kind.

(a) With the safety harness fitted to driver and passenger as previously described, start the engine and accelerate the vehicle to approximately 24 km/h (15 m.p.h.). Ensuring that it is safe to do so, brake sharply.

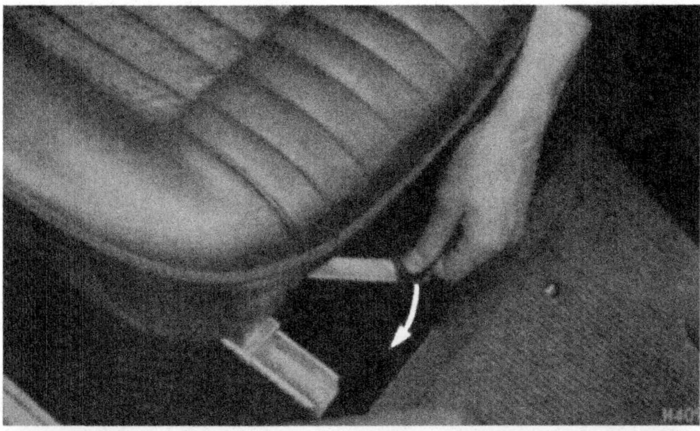

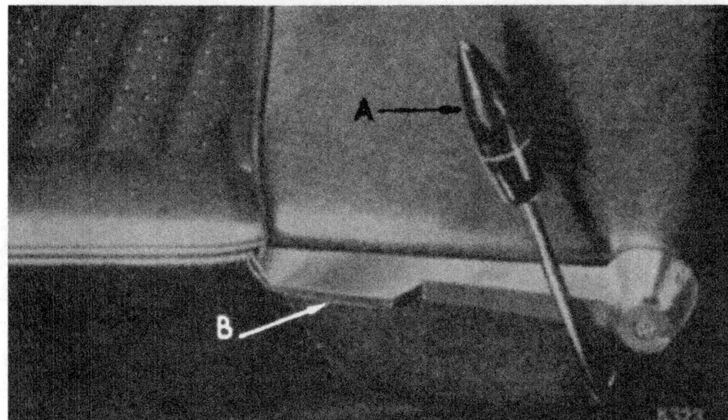

Fig. 1 (upper)   Fig. 2 (lower)

(b) The safety harness should automatically lock, holding both driver and passenger securely in position.

It is important when braking that the reaction of both driver and passenger is normal, i.e. the body must not be thrown forward in anticipation, thus causing a 'snatching' action of the reel which will not operate the locking mechanism. The harness is locked by retardation of the car, not by body movement.

SEATS

The seats are of the bucket type and have adjustable headrests to prevent the effects of backlash in an accident. The seats are pivoted at the front and secured at the rear by a spring loaded lever A (Fig. 2) which prevents the seat lifting during an accident. The lever, when moved forwards allows the seat to be tilted and access to be gained to the rear of the driving compartment.

To clean the seats refer to page 21 "Care of Bodywork".

Adjustments

The seats are adjustable for leg reach (fore and aft movement) and squab angle (back of the seat rake).

Leg reach adjustment

This is adjusted by moving the lever (Fig. 1) situated at the front of the seat and sliding the seat to the position required. Release the lever and try to slide the seat to ensure that the lever is correctly located and the seat is secure.

Squab angle adjustment

Sit in the seat, lift the lever B (Fig. 2) and assume the desired driving posture, the seat squab will automatically take up the correct position and the lever may be released.

LOCKS AND KEYS

Keys

The following keys are supplied with each new TR6.

3 Ignition keys.

2 Door keys.

2 Glove locker and trunk locker keys.

In addition, an ignition key identification disc is supplied and must be submitted to your Standard Triumph dealer when new ignition keys are required. As the disc is the only record of the ignition keys it should be kept in a safe place.

Door Locks

"Anti-burst" locks are fitted to both doors and are opened by a push button on the outside or by a remote control lever on the inside.

To lock a door from the inside, push the lever forward; to lock the door from the outside, insert the key and turn forward a quarter turn. To unlock a door turn the key rearward a quarter turn.

Ignition/Steering Lock and Key Warning System

See page 12 for operation.

Lubrication of Exterior Locks

Once a month, particularly in sub-zero temperatures, apply a few drops of light machine oil to the latch and key slots. Do not apply grease to lock cylinders.

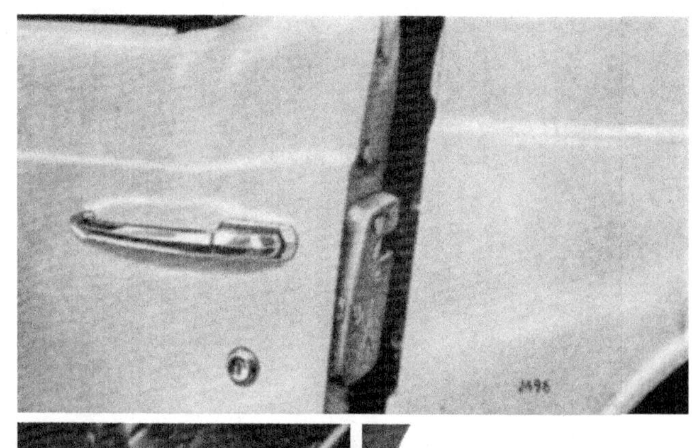

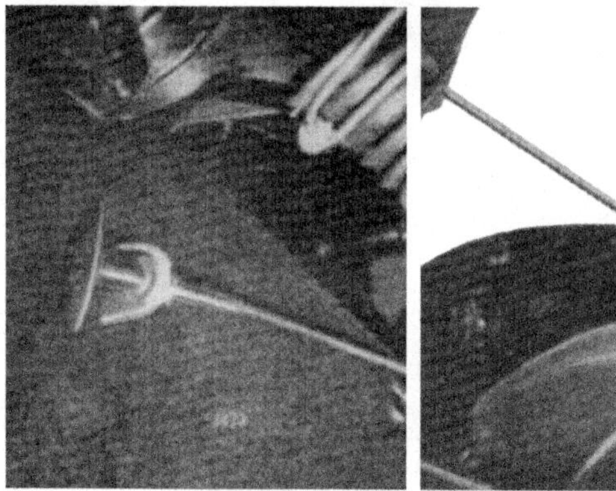

Fig. 1 (left)   Fig. 2 (upper)   Fig. 3 (right)

Fig. 4 (left)   **Fig. 5 (upper)**   **Fig. 6 (right)**

Bonnet Release (Fig. 1)

To open the bonnet pull the control situated below the left-hand side of the facia. The bonnet will rise sufficiently to enable the fingers to be inserted under the rear edge to give access to the safety catch. The bonnet can then be released and raised to a near vertical position, where it will be supported by a stay. Disengage the stay from its recess before attempting to close the bonnet.

Trunk Locker (Figs. 4 and 5)

To open the deck lid, depress the unlocked plunger (Fig. 5) and raise the lid to its limit before lowering it on to the telescopic support.

Close the lid by raising it slightly to release the catch (arrowed, Fig. 4) in the telescopic support, lower, and which may be locked, by turning the key a half turn counter-clockwise.

Fuel Filler Cap (Fig. 6)

The fuel filler cap, located forward of the trunk lid, is opened by lifting the catch at the side of the cap. Press the cap to close.

SOFT TOP

The soft top is made from P.V.C. material, and is supported by a hinged frame. The assembly folds down into the rear of the car and is protected by a soft top cover.

Lowering the Soft Top

Release the soft top header rail from the windshield frame by turning the catch levers in the direction as shown in Fig. 1.

Push the header rail, rearwards and slightly upwards, while knocking the soft side support (arrowed Fig. 2) downwards, until the assembly begins to fold. Continue lowering the frame and pull the fabric flat over the deck lid (Fig. 3).

Fold the fabric forwards over the soft top frame and turn the ends of the fabric inwards (Fig. 4). Ensure, that the Vybak windows are free from distortion and that the fabric is clear of the frame.

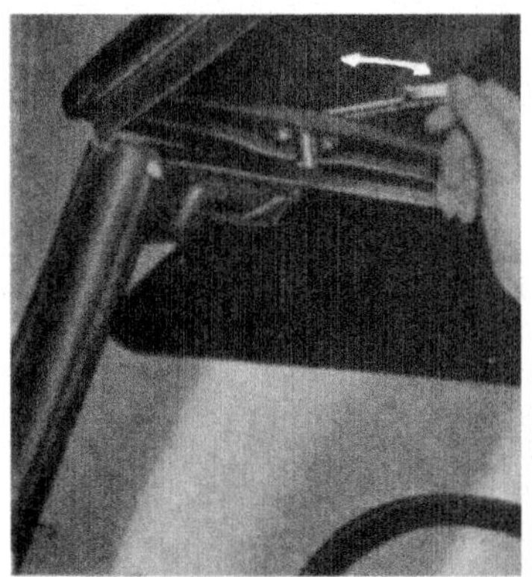

Fig. 1

Fig. 2

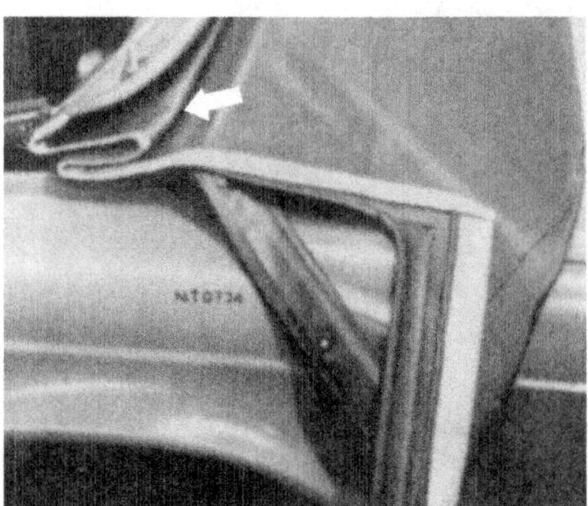

Fig. 3

Soft Top in the Down Position

Retain the soft top in position by fitting the cover as follows:

Attach the cover to the outer fasteners and continue working towards the center. Attach each strap to its respective fastener on the back wall of the floor well.

Raising the Soft Top

Unfasten and remove the soft top cover. Fold the sides of the fabric outwards and pull rearwards over the deck lid. Lifting the front header rail, raise the assembly sufficiently to allow the fabric to lie evenly over the soft top frame. Secure the fasteners (three each side, Fig. 5) to the body.

Secure the soft top header rail on the windshield frame, by turning the catch levers inwards towards the center of the car.

Opening backlight (Fig. 6)

To open the backlight, release the zip fastener and roll the panel downwards. Retain the rolled panel in position by attaching the straps to the press fasteners located on the back wall of the rear compartment.

Fig. 4

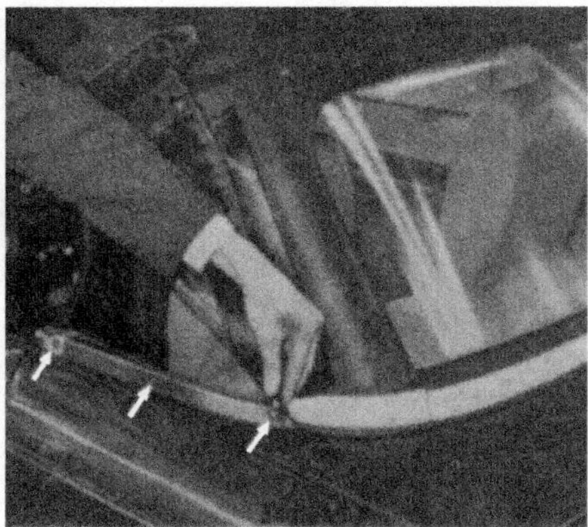

Fig. 5

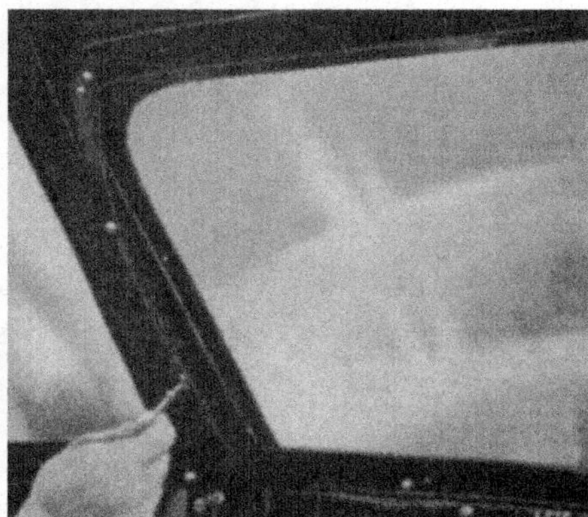

Fig. 6

Tonneau Cover (Optional)

The tonneau cover provides weather protection for the vehicle interior when the soft top is lowered. It incorporates press-studs for securing to the car and a zip fastener which permits access to either or both of the front seats.

Hard Top (Optional) (Figs. 7, 8, 9)

A hard top is available in kit form for fitment to soft top models, and may be removed and replaced as required.

Figs. 7 to 9 show the hard top attachments.

Fig. 7

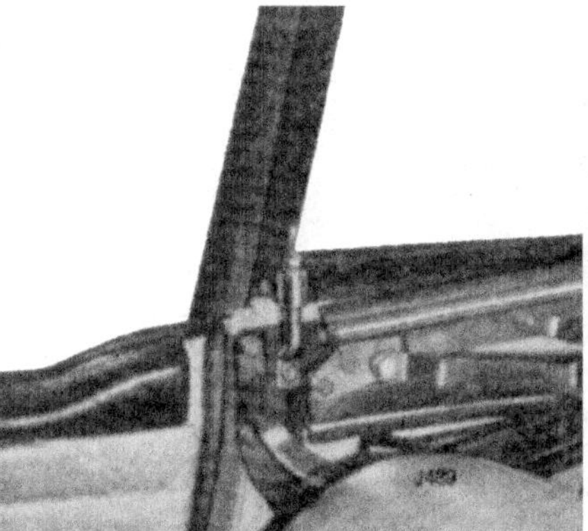

Fig. 8

Fig. 9

CARE OF BODYWORK

Washing

Avoid using a dry cloth to wipe dust from the paintwork and plated surfaces. Dust is an abrasive and if removed in this way it will scratch the polished surfaces. Wash the vehicle frequently with plenty of running water and a clean soft sponge. Soften and, if possible, remove the mud with water before using the sponge. When all dirt is removed, sponge off and dry with a clean damp chamois leather. Never wash or polish the vehicle under a hot sun.

Removing Grease and Tar

Remove grease or tar by sparing use of white spirit, but do not apply this to rubber, particularly windshield wiper brades.

Glass Surfaces

Glass is easily scratched. This can be avoided by always using a damp chamois leather which is specially reserved for use on glass only. If silicone polishes have been used on the body, take care that the polish does not come in contact with the glass. It is extremely difficult to remove and causes the windshield wipers to smear.

Chromium Plating

Frequent washing and thorough drying is recommended, especially during the winter months when there is likelihood of corrosion through contamination with road salt.

Polishing

After a period of use, the formation of traffic film will cause the paintwork to lose some of its lustre, even though the vehicle has been carefully and regularly washed. The original brilliance may be restored after washing by using a reputable non-abrasive cleaner and polish.

Being the most durable, wax preparations are preferable, but where these are used regularly the old wax must first be removed with a cleaner before further application of new wax. The frequency at which polishing is necessary will depend upon local conditions of air pollution.

Care of Interior, Soft Top and Tonneau Cover

Brush and clean the inside of your car each time you wash and polish the outside of it. Use a vacuum cleaner where possible and ensure complete removal of all dust from the interior and trim.

Wash the Upholstery (and exterior fabric) with luke-warm non-caustic soapy water. Do not use detergents or household cleaners as these may cause damage. Remove all traces of suds with a clean damp cloth and thoroughly dry the upholstery with a dry duster or towel.

Wipe the facia and instrument panel with a damp cloth only. Wax or other polishes should not be used inside the car.

Inflammability

The car conforms to State and Federal laws on flammability. To preserve this condition do not clean interior other than as described above.

Tires

Wheels and tires, of correct types and pressures, are an integral part of a vehicle's design. Thus the regular maintenance of the tires contributes not only to the safety but to the designed functioning of the vehicle, as road holding steering and braking are especially vulnerable to the use of incorrectly pressurised, badly fitted or worn tires.

Pressures

Adjust tire pressures in accordance with the recommendations given below. These pressures are satisfactory for sustained speeds up to 112 m.p.h. (180 km.h.).

	Front	Rear
185 SR-15 G800	20 lb/in.^{2}	24 lb/in.^{2}
185 SR-15 X	(1·41 kg/cm^2)	(1·69 kg/cm^2)

NOTE: Should the vehicle be tuned to increase its maximum speed, or be used for racing, consult the respective tire company regarding the need for tires of full racing construction.

Never bleed a warm tire but always adjust the pressure whilst the tires are cold, i.e. before a run. As the tires warm up their pressures will increase.

To prolong tire life, avoid severe braking, sudden changes of direction at speed, and driving over or against high kerbstones, as this can result in severe damage to the tire walls. Examine the tires occasionally and remove flints or other road matter which may have become embedded in the treads.

Cleaning

Wipe off any oil or grease which may be on the tires by using a cloth moistened in gasoline. The tires should then be washed, using only soap and water.

Tire Wear

The characteristics of tires vary considerably and, therefore when new tires are fitted, all four tires must be of the same type and rating. (185–15 radial ply).

Occasionally remove flints and other road matter from the treads and examine the tires for sharp fins, flats and other irregularities. An upstanding sharp fin on the edge of each pattern rib is a sure sign of road wheel misalignment (Fig. 1).

Fins on the inside of the pattern ribs indicate toe-in. Fins on the outside edges indicate toe-out. Sharp pattern edges may also be caused by road camber, even when wheel alignment is correct. In such cases, it is better to make sure by having the track checked with an alignment gauge.

"Spotty" tread wear or flats, can result from grabbing brakes or unbalanced wheel assemblies. Your Triumph Dealer will check the action of the brakes and re-balance the tires if required. The original degree of balance is not necessarily maintained, and it may be affected by uneven tread wear, by repairs, by tire removal and refitting, or by wheel damage and eccentricities. The vehicle may also become more sensitive to unbalance due to normal wear of moving parts.

Excessive wear in the center of the tread (Fig. 2) results from over-inflation, in which condition the fabric is more easily damaged.

Excessive wear at the outer edge of the tread (Fig. 3) results from under-inflation, a condition which causes excessive heating and premature tire failure.

Wheel Changing Procedure (Pressed Steel Wheels)
1. Place the vehicle on firm, level, ground if this is not possible exercise extreme caution.
2. Apply the handbrake.

3. Remove the spare wheel from below the luggage compartment floor (Fig. 5).
4. Check the spare wheel pressure and ensure that it is correct (i.e. Front 20 p.s.i. or Rear 24 p.s.i.).
5. With the tool provided slightly slacken the wheel nuts (Fig. 4.)
6. Locate the head of the jack under a chassis member (rearward of the front wheel or forwards of the rear wheel (Fig. 6). Assemble the handle into the jack and turn to lift the wheel clear of the ground.

Fig. 1   Fig. 2   Fig. 3

Fig. 4

Fig. 5 (upper)   Fig. 6 (lower)

7. Remove the wheel nuts and hub trim (Fig. 7) and lift off wheel.

8. Fit spare wheel and hub trim plate securing with wheel nuts. Ensure that the wheel nuts tighten without trapping the hub trim.

9. Lower wheel and remove jack.

10. Tighten wheel nuts securely and ensure that the wheel nuts are correctly positioned when fully tightened.

11. Stow tools and spare wheel in luggage compartment.

Fig. 7

COOLING SYSTEM

The pressurised "no less" cooling system incorporates a translucent plastic overflow reservoir (Fig. 2) which collects excess coolant from the radiator as the coolant in the system expands with heat. Depression created as the system cools, causes the coolant to flow back from the reservoir into the radiator. The fluid level, which is visible through the translucent reservoir, should be maintained at least half full when cold.

Draining

To drain the system, move the heat control (23) page 10 to the hot position, lift the bonnet and disconnect the water hose at the bottom right hand side of the radiator before removing the radiator cap (Fig. 1).

CAUTION: If the engine is hot, avoid danger from scalding by exercising extreme care when removing the radiator filler cap. Turn it a half-turn and allow pressure to be fully released before completely removing the cap.

Flushing

Efficient cooling is maintained by thoroughly flushing the system once each year before adding anti-freeze. When carrying this out, it is advantageous to remove the bottom hose and to use plenty of clean running water.

Allowing anti-freeze solution to remain in the system throughout the summer period affords anti-corrosion protection. The solution, however, should be checked at the beginning of each winter period as the inhibitor becomes exhausted. See Page 27.

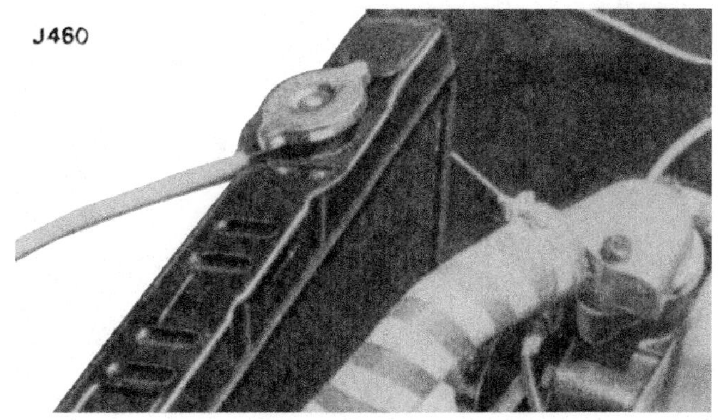

Fig. 1

Filling

Reconnect the bottom radiator hose, open the heat control (23) page 10 and remove the radiator cap (Fig. 1). Fill the cooling system with clean (soft) water and run the engine at approximately 1,500 r.p.m. for one or two minutes. Stop the engine and top up the radiator. Replace the radiator cap and half fill the plastic overflow reservoir with clean (soft) water.

Fig. 2 (upper)   **Fig. 3 (lower)**

Windshield Washer (Fig. 3)

Examine the water level in the plastic windshield washer container. If required, unscrew the cap and replenish the container with clean water. Under freezing conditions, fill the container with a mixture of methylated spirits (alcohol) and water, the recommended proportions being 1 part alcohol to 2 parts water. This may then be used to disperse ice and snow from the windshield. Do not use anti-freeze solution in the windshield washer as this may discolor the paintwork and damage the wiper blades and sealing rubber.

Frost Precautions

The car heater cannot be completely drained by normal methods. Therefore frost damage will not be prevented by merely draining the radiator.

For your protection during freezing weather, an approved anti-freeze solution should be added to the coolant in the radiator.

Because of the searching effect of these solutions, advise your dealer to check the system for leaks before adding the anti-freeze.

At certain temperatures glycol water solutions adopt a "mushy" state with a viscosity which impairs circulation and can immobilise or damage the water pump. Therefore, consult the following chart before adding anti-freeze, for the degree of frost protection required.

ANTI-FREEZE CONCENTRATION		25%	30%	35%	50%
SPECIFIC GRAVITY OF COOLANT AT 15.5°C (60°F)		1.039	1.048	1.054	1.076
ANTI-FREEZE QUANTITY	PINTS IMP.	2.8	3.3	3.9	5.5
	PINTS U.S.A.	3.4	4.0	4.7	6.6
	LITRES	2.0	2.3	2.7	3.8
DEGREE OF PROTECTION	**Complete** Car may be driven away immediately from cold	−12°C 10°F	−16°C 3°F	−20°C −4°F	−36°C −33°F
	Safe Limit Coolant in mushy state. Engine may be started and driven away after short warm-up period	−18°C 0°F	−22°C −8°F	−28°C −18°F	−41°C −42°F
	Lower Protection Prevents frost damage to cylinder head, block and radiator. Thaw out before starting engine.	−26°C −15°F	−32°C −26°F	−37°C −35°F	−47°C −53°F

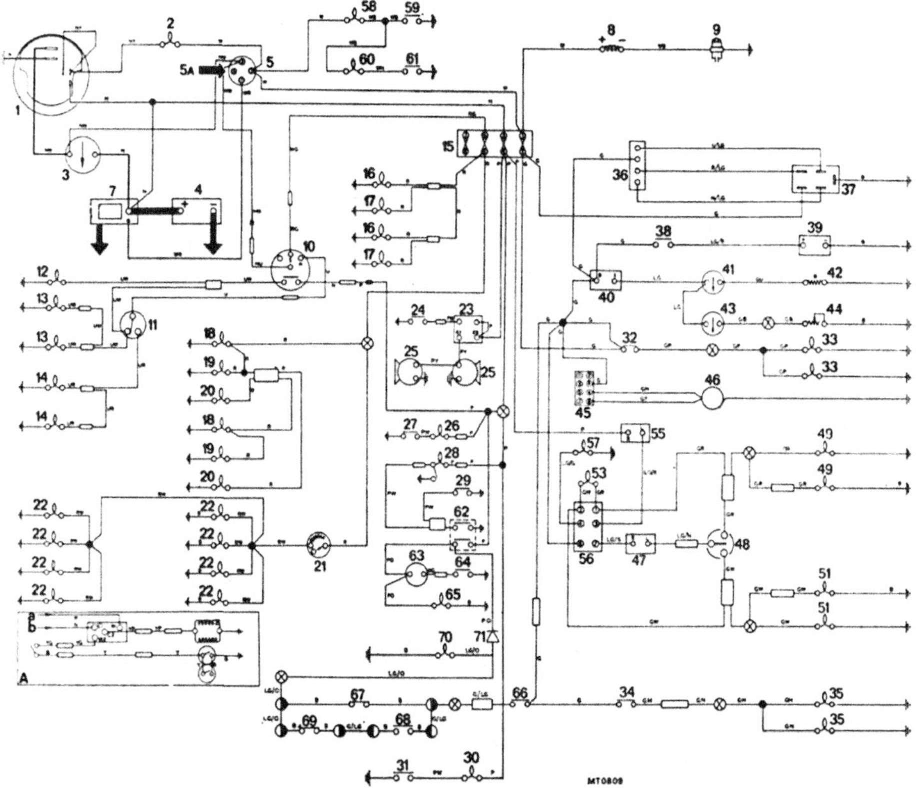

Fig. 1 Wiring Diagram

KEY TO WIRING DIAGRAM

CAUTION: THIS VEHICLE IS FITTED WITH A NEGATIVE EARTH ELECTRICAL SYSTEM. ENSURE THAT THE BATTERY EARTH LEAD IS ALWAYS CONNECTED TO THE BATTERY NEGATIVE TERMINAL.

THE ALTERNATOR—AND POSSIBLY SOME ACCESSORIES—CONTAIN POLARITY SENSITIVE COMPONENTS THAT MAY BE IRREPARABLY DAMAGED IF SUBJECTED TO INCORRECT POLARITY.

1	Alternator	26	Cubby box illumination	53	Turn signal warning light
2	Ignition warning light	27	Cubby box illumination switch		
3	Ammeter	28	Transmission tunnel lamp	55	Hazard flasher unit
4	Battery	29	R.H. door switch	56	Hazard switch
5	Ignition/starter switch	30	Luggage boot lamp	57	Hazard warning light
5A	Ignition/starter switch— radio supply connector	31	Luggage boot lamp switch	58	Brake line failure warning light
		32	Stop lamp switch	59	Brake line failure switch
		33	Stop lamp	60	Oil pressure warning light
7	Starter motor	34	Reverse lamp switch	61	Oil pressure switch
8	Ignition coil	35	Reverse lamp	62	L.H. door switch
9	Ignition distributor	36	Windscreen wiper switch	63	Buzzer
10	Column light switch	37	Windscreen wiper motor	64	Key switch
11	Dip switch	38	Windscreen washer switch	65	Key light
12	Main beam warning light	39	Windscreen washer pump	66	Belt warning gearbox switch
13	Main beam	40	Voltage stabilizer	67	Drivers belt switch
14	Dip beam	41	Temperature indicator	68	Passengers seat switch
15	Fuse box	42	Temperature transmitter	69	Passengers belt switch
16	Front parking lamp	43	Fuel indicator	70	Belt warning light
17	Front marker lamp	44	Fuel tank unit	71	Diode
18	Rear marker lamp	45	Heater switch		
19	Tail lamp	46	Heater motor		
20	Plate illumination lamp	47	Turn signal flasher unit		
21	Panel rheostat	48	Turn signal switch		
22	Instrument illumination	49	L.H. Flasher lamp		
23	Horn relay				
24	Horn push	51	R.H. Flasher lamp		
25	Horn				

COLOUR CODE

N.	Brown	LG.	Light Green
U.	Blue	W.	White
R.	Red	Y.	Yellow
P.	Purple	S.	Slate
G.	Green	B.	Black

FUSE SYSTEM

The fuse box is mounted on the left-hand side of the engine bay. The unit contains three operational fuses, one fuse available for use to protect an accessory circuit and has provision to house two spares. The fuses are protected by a pull-off cover.

Failure of a particular fuse is indicated when all the circuits protected by it become inoperative. If a new fuse fails establish the cause and rectify the fault before fitting a second replacement.

Fuse

Manufacturer..	..	..	Lucas
Rating	..	..	35 amp.
Lucas Part No.	..	..	188218
Stanpart No. ..	..	..	58465

Circuits

The top fuse is not used on a standard production vehicle.

Fig. 2

It may be employed in service to protect an accessory circuit.

The fuse fed by a white cable from the ignition/starter switch protects the following circuits:

Stop lamp
Reverse lamp
Windscreen wiper
Windscreen washer
Temperature indication
Fuel indication
Heater
Turn signal
Seat belt warning

The fuse fed by a brown cable from the battery protects the following circuits:

Horn
Headlamp flasher
Cubby box illumination
Key warning
Courtesy light
Hazard warning
Transmission tunnel lamp
Luggage boot lamp

The fuse fed by a red/green cable from the column light switch protects the following circuits:

Front parking lamp
Front marker lamp
Rear marker lamp
Tail lamp
Plate illumination lamp
Instrument illumination

CHARGING SYSTEM

CAUTION: THE ALTERNATOR CONTAINS POLARITY SENSITIVE COMPONENTS. REFER TO "CAUTION" ON PAGE 29.

DO NOT MAKE OR BREAK ANY CONNECTIONS IN THE CHARGING CIRCUIT—INCLUDING THE BATTERY LEADS—WHILE THE ENGINE IS RUNNING OR DAMAGE TO COMPONENTS MAY OCCUR. THE ALTERNATOR MUST ONLY BE RUN WITH ALL THE CHARGING CIRCUIT CONNECTIONS MADE OR WITH THE ALTERNATOR MULTI-SOCKET CONNECTORS DISCONNECTED.

Alternator

The Lucas 17ACR alternator—which contains its own control unit—is driven by a vee belt which should be adjusted as detailed on page 57. The field winding rotor runs on two "lubricated for life" ball bearings. (No routine lubrication is required).

Ignition Warning Light

The three "field winding supply" diodes enable a circuit similar to a conventional generator warning light circuit to be employed. If the warning light remains illuminated during normal running a fault is indicated.

BATTERY

CAUTION: REFER TO "CAUTIONS" ON PAGES 29 AND 33.

A conventional battery is located on the bulkhead. Battery data is given on page 71.

Ensure that the battery top and terminals remain clean and dry. Coat terminals with petroleum jelly (Vaseline) to prevent corrosion.

Check electrolyte level monthly and if required replenish with pure water as detailed on page 51. If electrolyte has been spilled clean the affected area with a cloth moistened with ammonia to neutralize the acid and prevent acid corrosion.

Ensure that the battery is always firmly clamped in position by the retaining assembly. When fitting battery leads do not hammer terminals to terminal posts. Such action may damage battery.

The battery will deteriorate rapidly if left in a discharged condition. If the unit is reduced to a low state of charge it should be recharged at the first opportunity.

BULB CHART

Light	Watts	Lucas Part No.	Stanpart No.	
Headlights				
R.H. Dip—U.S.A.	50/40	54522231	——	*
France	45/40	411	510219	
Other R.H. Dip markets ..	60/50	54523079	215735	*
L.H. Dip	60/45	54521872	512231	*
Front parking and flasher lamps	5/21	380	502287	
Front marker lamps	4	222	501436	
Rear marker lamps	4	222	501436	
Rear flasher lamps	21	382	502379	
Tail/stop lamps	5/21	380	502287	
Reverse lamps	21	382	502379	
Plate illumination lamps	6	207	57591	
Luggage boot lamp	3	256	57599	
Transmission tunnel lamp	6	254	59897	
Courtesy light	2·2	987	59492	
Cubby box illumination	2·2	987	59492	
Instrument illumination	2·2	987	59492	
Warning lights	2·2	987	59492	
Seat belt warning light	2	281	513000	

* Sealed beam light units.

HEADLAMPS

NOTE: TO AVOID BEAM AIMING DO NOT DISTURB BEAM AIMING SCREWS A AND B.

Beam Aiming

Insert a large screwdriver behind rim adjacent to clip as shown on Fig. 3. Twist screwdriver to release rim from clip. Lift rim from upper retainers. Screw A positions the beam in the horizontal plane. Screw B controls beam height.

Beam aiming can best be accomplished using equipment such as Lucas "Beamsetter" or "Lev-L-Lite". This service is available at Triumph distributors or dealers and will ensure maximum road illumination with minimum discomfort to other road users.

Filament Failure

In the event of a filament failure the sealed beam light unit must be replaced. Insert a large screwdriver behind rim adjacent to clip as shown on Fig. 3. Twist screwdriver to release rim from clip. Lift rim from upper retainers. Remove three screws 1, 2 and 3 (Fig. 4) to release retaining rim and sealed beam light unit. Pull connector from light unit (Fig. 5). Renew light unit and reassemble.

Fig. 3

Fig. 4

Fig. 5

LAMPS—BULB RENEWAL

Bulb renewal for the majority of lamps is conventional.
Remove lens by unscrewing required screw/screws. Renew bulb
and re-assemble.

Interior Lamp

Located under the passenger side facia and secured to the facia by a plastic clip. Disengage the lamp from the clip, and remove the bulb by pressing it towards the holder and turning it a quarter turn.

Instrument Illumination and Warning Lamps

Working from behind the instrument, pull bulb holder—which is a component of the main harness—from instrument. Unscrew bulb from holder, renew bulb and reassemble.

Note that the speedometer and tachometer each have two illumination bulbs.

Key Illumination Lamp

Located near the ignition/starter key lock.
Remove the bulb holder from its securing bracket by upwards pressure and unscrew the bulb anti-clockwise.

Brake Failure and Seat Belt Warning Indicators

Should difficulty be experienced in reaching the rear of the lamp to replace a bulb, the lamp itself may be carefully prized out from the facia, using a suitable tool.

Cubby Box Illumination (Fig. 6)

Open cubby box lid. Carefully unscrew bulb from holder. Renew bulb.

Luggage Boot Lamp (Fig. 7)

Open luggage boot lid. Detach lens and base by removing two screws. Renew festoon bulb and reassemble.

Rear marker, rear flasher, tail/stop and reverse lamps (Fig. 8)

Open luggage boot lid. Remove carpet, Remove spare wheel cover. Remove six screws and withdraw appropriate trim panel. Pull appropriate bulb holder from lamp base. Renew bulb and reassemble.

Fig. 6

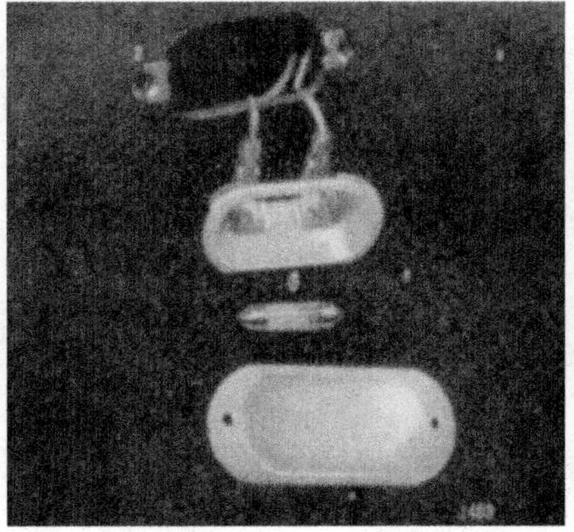

Fig. 7

Fig. 8

TURN SIGNAL FLASHER UNIT—RENEWAL

Locate unit attached to clip secured to bulkhead end panel adjacent to passengers feet. Pull unit from clip. Disconnect electrical connectors. Connect electrical connectors to new unit and insert into clip.

Fig. 9

KEY WARNING SYSTEM

This system is designed to encourage the driver to remove the ignition key from the lock before leaving the vehicle. The system should prevent encouragement of theft but is not intended as a comprehensive anti-theft device.

If the driver's door is opened while the ignition key is in the lock an audible buzzer will sound. Removing the key or closing the door will cause the buzzing to cease.

The buzzer is housed in a cylindrical container located adjacent to the courtesy light.

Associated with the key warning system is the courtesy light which illuminates the lock to facilitate key entry and the transmission tunnel lamp. The left-hand door switch contains two individual contact sets. One set controls the supply to the buzzer and courtesy light while the second set provides an earth return for the transmission tunnel lamp circuit. The single function right-hand door switch provides an earth return for the transmission tunnel lamp circuit. Refer to wiring diagram for full circuit information.

Starting the Engine from Cold

Check, and if necessary top up, the radiator water level and the engine oil level. If the car has not been used for several days and fuel has evaporated from the carburetors, refill them by operating the priming lever on the fuel pump. The slight resistance ceases when the float chambers are full.

Apply the handbrake and ensure that the gear shift lever is in the "Neutral" position. In cold weather pull the choke control fully out; in warm weather pull to the mid-position. In hot climates, do not use the control. Insert the ignition key and turn it to the "Ignition" position, causing the "no charge", "low oil pressure" and "brake failure" indicator lights to glow, the fuel gauge to register the contents of the fuel tank and the temperature gauge to register the temperature of the engine coolant.

From the "Ignition" position, turn the key clockwise against spring pressure to operate the starter motor. Immediately the engine fires, release the key, which will return to the "Ignition" position. Should the engine fail to start at the first attempt, do not re-operate the starter switch until the starter motor has come to rest.

As soon as the engine starts, push the choke control "half in" (cold climates), or "fully in" (warm climates) and warm the engine at an idling speed of approximately 1,500 r.p.m. This will cause the "no charge", "low oil pressure" and "brake failure" indicator lights to be extinguished, thus indicating satisfactory performance of the generating, lubricating and braking systems. Should an indicator light remain on, stop the engine and establish the cause. Failure to do so may result in serious damage.

After starting the engine, cylinder wear is minimised if the engine is warmed up quickly by driving away when the indicator lights are extinguished. Maintain an engine speed of approximately 1,500 r.p.m. until the choke control can be pushed fully in. In warm climates, use of the control may be unnecessary. Avoid the use of full throttle during the warming-up period. A thermostat incorporated in the cooling system enables the engine to be warmed up quickly from cold.

Starting a Hot Engine

When re-starting a hot engine, depress the throttle pedal to about one-third of its travel before operating the starter switch. The choke control should not be used.

Running-in

The importance of correct running-in cannot be too strongly emphasised, for during the first few thousand miles of motoring, the working surfaces of a new engine are bedding down.

When driving from new, avoid placing heavy loads upon the engine, such as using full throttle at low speeds or when the engine is cold. Running-in should be progressive, and no harm will result from the engine being allowed to "rev" fairly fast for short periods provided that it is thoroughly warm and not pulling hard. Always select a lower gear if necessary to relieve the engine of load.

Full power should not be used until at least 1,000 miles (1,600 km.) have been covered and even then, it should be used only for short periods at a time. These periods can be extended as the engine becomes more responsive.

Recommended Speed Limits

Owners are advised not to drive the car at engine speeds over 5,800 r.p.m., indicated by the beginning of the red segment on the tachometer, and to avoid over-revving, particularly in the lower gears.

Recommended Fuel

The "TR6" engine is designed to operate on fuels having a minimum octane rating of 91 (Research Method).

See Emmission Control System, page 42.

Overdrive Unit (when fitted)

An overdrive unit serves as a convenient method of providing, at will, a numerically lower overall gear ratio to reduce engine speed and wear, and to effect fuel economy.

Greatest benefit will accrue from judicious use of the overdrive, the governing factor being that the vehicle continues to run easily without sign of engine laboring, combined with the minimum amount of throttle opening necessary to maintain this condition.

Do not change from overdrive at engine speeds in excess of 4,000 r.p.m. This corresponds approximately with perak revs. in normal gears. Damage can result from overdrive disengagement at higher engine speed.

ROUTINE SERVICING

The lubricants listed on page 67, have maintained a high standard of quality over many years and are approved only after extensive tests in collaboration with the oil companies concerned. In countries where these oils are unabtainable, use similar oils having the same characteristics. The use of only high grade lubricants is vitally important and cannot be over-emphasised.

Engine

When a new car is delivered, the engine oil pan contains a quantity of special oil, sufficient for the running-in period. Should the level fall below the low mark on the dipstick, the oil pan may be topped-up with any of the approved lubricants.

At the "Free Service", the running-in oil is drained and the oil pan replenished to the level of the high mark on the dipstick, with one of the approved oils.

Transmission, Overdrive and Rear Axle

Rear axles, transmission and overdrive units fitted to new cars are filled with a special oil, formulated to give all necessary protection to new gears. This oil should not be drained but may be topped up with any of the approved oils.

Braking System

In addition to adjustment and examination/renewal of shoes and pads at the intervals recommended in the following pages, it is strongly recommended that the brake fluid be renewed and that the braking system be overhauled every 36,000 miles (60,000 km.) or 3 years (whichever is the sooner).

Overhauling the brake system involves dismantling, examining and renewal of all seals and defective items.

Owners are urged to seek the assistance of any Triumph Distributor or Dealer who will be pleased to estimate for the work which is of such a nature that it should be entrusted only to skilled workshop personnel.

Preventive Maintenance

To ensure continued efficiency and prolonged vehicle life, the Maintenance Schedule produced by Triumph engineers, offers a carefully designed plan of lubrication requirements and adjustment checks at pre-determined periods.

Operated by all Triumph dealers, and specifically recommended to owners wishing to obtain the greatest pleasure from their motoring, the plan involves the use of a series of Maintenance Vouchers contained in this booklet supplied with the car. Service operations appropriate to mileage or periods of time are also listed.

The space provided on the counterfoil of each voucher should be filled in by the dealer to constitute proof of regular servicing, should this be required when making a claim under the warranty, or when selling the vehicle.

MAINTENANCE SUMMARY

Interval in miles × 1,000 : **3 · 6 · 12**
Interval in Kilometres × 1,000 : **5 · 10 · 20**

DESCRIPTION	3 / 5	6 / 10	12 / 20
ENGINE COMPARTMENT			
Check/top up engine oil level	×		
Check/top up cooling system	×	×	×
Check/top up brake fluid reservoir	×	×	×
Check/top up clutch fluid reservoir	×	×	×
Check/top up windscreen fluid reservoir	×	×	×
Check/top up battery	×	×	×
Check/top up carburetter piston(s) damper(s) (E)		×	×
Drain engine oil and refill		×	×
Renew oil filter element			×
Clean fuel pump sediment bowl and filter gauze			×
Lubricate distributor and check automatic advance (E)		×	×
Check/adjust/report condition of distributor points (E)		×	
Renew distributor points (E)			×
Check/adjust ignition timing using electronic equipment (E)		×	×
Check/report ignition wiring for fraying, chafing and deterioration (E)		×	×
Check condenser and coil for breakdown on oscilascope tune (E)		×	×
Clean/adjust sparking plugs (E)		×	
Renew sparking plugs (E)			×
Check/adjust torque of cylinder head nuts/bolts (E)			×
Check/report cylinder compression (E)		×	×
Check/adjust valve rocker clearances (E)			×
Clean engine oil filler cap			×
Clean carburetter air cleaner element(s) (E)		×	
Renew carburetter air cleaner element(s) (E)			×
Check/adjust/report condition of all driving belts	×	×	×
Check security of starter motor and alternator retaining bolts			
Check security of engine mountings			
Check/adjust carburetter settings (E)		×	×
Overhaul carburetter—at 24,000 miles (E)			
Renew fuel line filter (E)			×
Check fuel system for leaks (E)	×	×	×
Lubricate accelerator linkage/pedal fulcrum and check operation		×	×
Check battery condition; Clean and grease connections		×	×
Check/report for oil/fuel/fluid leaks (general) (E)	×	×	×
Check/report leaks from cooling and heater systems	×	×	×

Interval in miles × 1,000 : **3 · 6 · 12**
Interval in Kilometres × 1,000 : **5 · 10 · 20**

DESCRIPTION	3 / 5	6 / 10	12 / 20
ENGINE COMPARTMENT (continued)			
Evaporative and crankcase ventilation systems:—			
Check hoses and restrictors for blockage, security and deterioration (E)		×	×
Renew carbon cannister at 24,000 miles (E)			
UNDERBODY			
Check/top up level of gearbox (and overdrive) oil		×	×
Check/top up level of final drive unit oil		×	×
Lubricate lower steering swivel		×	×
Lubricate all grease points except hubs		×	×
Lubricate steering rack and pinion		×	×
Lubricate handbrake linkage and cable guides		×	×
Lubricate exposed automatic transmission selector linkages			×
Check engine, transmission, final drive, suspension and steering unit for oil leaks and report	×		
Check visually brake, clutch and fuel pipes, hoses and unions for chaffing leaks and corrosion and report	×	×	×
Check/report exhaust system for leakage and security (E)	×	×	×
Check security of suspension fixings, tie rod levers, steering unit attachments and steering universal joint coupling bolts			×
Check security of propeller shaft and drive shaft universal coupling bolts and report drive shaft gaiter condition			×
Check security of sub-frame or body mountings			
Check/report condition of steering unit/steering joints for security backlash and gaiter condition	×	×	×
EXTERIOR			
Adjust front hubs			×
Check /adjust front and rear wheel alignment with tracking equipment			×
Check/report front and rear wheel alignment with tracking equipment		×	×
Inspect brake pads for wear and discs for condition	×	×	×
Inspect and report brake linings for wear and drums for condition			×
Renew hydraulic brake fluid at 18,000 miles (or 3 years)			
At 36,000 miles (or 3 years):—			
Examine Brake, clutch and power steering systems seals and hoses and renew if necessary			

Interval in miles ×1,000	3	6	12
Interval in Kilometres ×1,000	5	10	20

DESCRIPTION

EXTERIOR (continued)

Description	3	6	12
Examine working surfaces of pistons and bores in master, slave and wheel cylinders and renew pats where necessary ..			
Renew air filter in brake servo unit			
Renew all water hoses			
Check/adjust security of road wheel fastenings	×	×	×
Check that tyres are in accordance with manufacturer's specification	×	×	×
Check visually and report depth of tread, cuts in tyre fabric, exposure of ply or cord structure, lumps or bulges	×	×	×
Check/adjust tyre pressures (including spare wheel)	×	×	×
Check/adjust headlamp alignment			
Check/report headlamp alignment	×	×	×
Check, if necessary replace, windscreen wiper blades	×	×	×
Check fuel tank filler cap seal for security (E)		×	×
*Important—If the tyres do not conform with legal requirements report to the owner			

Interval in miles ×1,000	3	6	12
Interval in Kilometres ×1,000	5	10	20

DESCRIPTION

INTERIOR

Description	3	6	12
Check brake pedal travel and handbrake operation, adjust if necessary			
Check/report brake pedal travel and handbrake operation ..	×	×	×
Check operation of window controls, locks and bonnet release ..			
Check function of all electrical systems and windscreen washer ..	×	×	×
Lubricate brake and clutch pedal pivots		×	×
Lubricate all locks, door hinges, strikers and bonnet release ..		×	×
Check/report condition and security of seats and seat belts ..	×	×	×
Check/report rear view mirrors for looseness, cracks and crazing	×	×	×

ROAD TEST

Description	3	6	12
Road/roller test and report additional work required		×	×
Ensure cleanliness of controls, door handles, steering wheel, etc.	×	×	×

All Triumph models entering the North American markets incorporate efficient emission control systems. These systems enable the vehicles to conform with all current State and Federal Regulations governing the emission of hydrocarbons, carbon monoxide, nitric oxide and the emission of fuel, by evaporation, from the fuel delivery system.

Fuel

The TR6 (U.S.A.) performs efficiently on fuels by 91 octane (Research method). **Note:** The engine is not designed to use unleaded fuel, and whilst the occasional tankful will not cause damage, constant use of unleaded fuels will result in excessive wear which will affect the emission control system.

Special Features

1. Crankcase breathing and evacuation of 'blow by' gases is achieved by utilizing the characteristic partial vacuum in the constant depression carburetters. But by this method crankcase emissions are burned in the engine combustion process. A wire gauze strainer in the engine top cover acts as an oil separator/flame trap.

2. The twin carburetters are Stromberg 175 CDSE(V) which are designed to be highly efficient and sensitive to varying conditions. The following features are incorporated:

   (a) Jet assembly and needle biased to achieve consistent air to fuel ratio.

   (b) Temperature compensator assembly which progressively opens in line with the engine temperature to correct the mixture and maintain even running.

   (c) Throttle by-pass valve which is set to open at a predetermined manifold depression to admit air during deceleration.

   (d) 'Free movement' built into the accelerator linkage permits fast idle without disturbing the otherwise closed position of the linkage.

   (e) Sealed cover to discourage unauthorized tampering.

3. The evaporative control system uses activated a carbon filter through which the fuel tank is vented. The following are features of the evaporative control system (Fig. 5).

   (1) The carburetter float chambers are vented to the engine during open throttle conditions and to the carbon canister at closed throttle.

   (2) The carbon canister (Fig. 1) is vented to atmosphere via an anti-run on valve. The canister is purged and prevented from vapour build-up by piping to the constant depression area of each carburetter. The crankcase breathing is also linked to the above piping system via the right-hand cam cover.

   (3) A separator tank prevents fuel surges from reaching the canister and thus saturating the system.

   (4) The fuel filter cap is sealed to prevent evaporative losses.

   (5) The fuel tank filler tube extends into the tank to prevent complete filling and so allow for expansion of fuel in hot weather.

   (6) The piping from the separator tank to canister contains a restrictor valve which will prevent the fuel tank being overfilled.

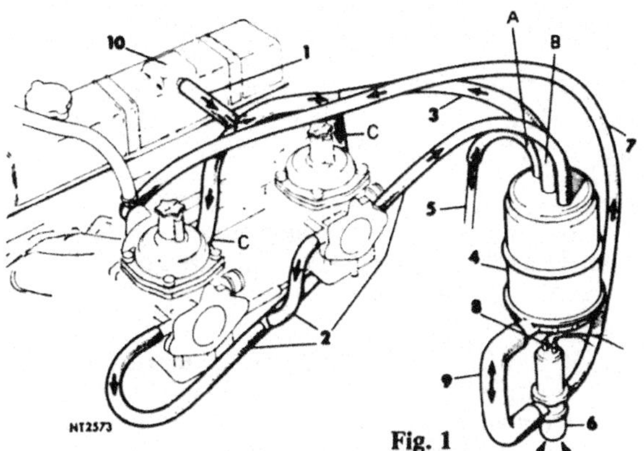

Fig. 1

1 Crankcase Breather pipe
2 Vent valve connecting pipes
3 Canister purge pipe
4 Evaporative control canister
5 Canister to fuel tank pipe
6 Run-on control valve
7 Vacuum control pipe
8 Solenoid connections
9 Canister to run-on control valve pipe
10 Flame arrestor
A 1/32 in. restrictor
B 3/32 in. restrictor
C 5/16 in. restrictors

4. A Thermostatic vacuum switch (Fig. 2) prevents overheating during prolonged idling, by increasing the speed of the engine, thus promoting more efficient cooling at high ambient temperatures.

System Description

A valve, located in the cooling system, is connected in the vacuum pipe, carburettor to distributor. A sensor in the coolant vents the vacuum pipe and atmosphere at 105°C (220°F). The effect is to negate the retard system, thus advancing the timing of the ignition spark and increasing the engine speed.

Servicing

No routine servicing of the system is required other than a visual check of the piping.

5. The anti-run-on valve prevents the 'running-on' of the engine after the ignition is switched off when, due to the heat of the engine, a condition of compression ignition is set up.
The method of achieving a cut off is by applying a slight 'vacuum' to the float chamber of the carburettors when the ignition is switched off.

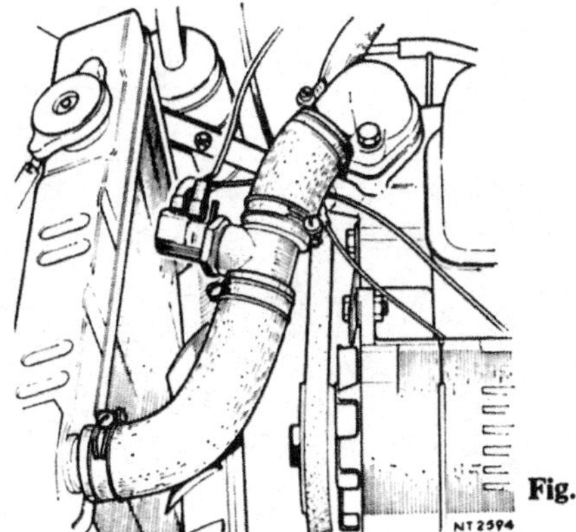

Fig. 2

System Description

When the ignition is switched off a solenoid is activated which operates a valve that seals off the inlet to the bottom of the carbon cannister. With the inlet sealed a connection to the inlet manifold applies a partial vacuum to the cannister and consequently to the float chambers via an interconnecting pipe. The vacuum thus applied is sufficient to prevent fuel being drawn into the engine. When the engine has stopped and the oil pressure drops to zero the solenoid is deactivated and the engine is thus ready again for operation.

Servicing

The system requires no servicing other than checking for deterioration and safe connection of the system piping.

Function Checks

If the engine is not working then it will be apparent by the running-on of the engine. A system check can be made by applying current to the solenoid which, if working correctly, will stop the engine.

EMISSION CONTROL SYSTEM—SERVICING

The importance of servicing at the correct intervals cannot be overstressed as improvements in design and manufacturing techniques count for nothing if the servicing standards are not upheld.

Routine servicing, carried out at the mileage intervals quoted in the Maintenance Summary will prevent any deterioration to the system. In addition to normal lubrication and nut tightness checks, those items which should receive attention during routine servicing include: distributor maintenance, carburetter dash-pot oil replenishment and slow running adjustment, spark plus, valve clearances, air cleaner, crankcase ventilation and fuel filter.

Ignition Distributor, refer to page 72 for ignition timing.

To assist in the location of faults in the system a trouble tracing chart is given on page 47.

Compression Check

Use a comparison type pressure gauge to check the compression pressure of each cylinder. Maximum variation over eight cylinders 5 lb/in^2 (0.35 kg/cm^2).

EVAPORATION CONTROL SYSTEM—SERVICING

Minimal servicing is required on the evaporation control system apart from renewing the carbon canister and checking visually the security of piping on the system.

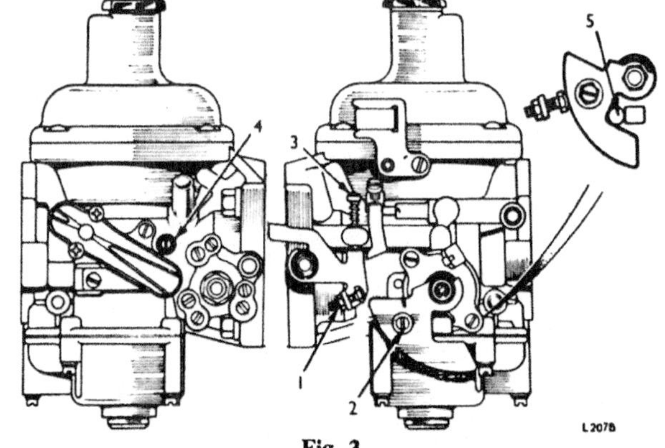

Fig. 3

CARBURETTERS

The twin Stromberg CDSE(V) 175 emission carburetters are the prime components of the emission system and great care is exercised during the manufacture and initial adjustment of these instruments. Because of the precise manufacturing limits involved and the assembly methods adopted to prevent unauthorized tampering during use, the extent of permissible servicing is restricted to the following:

Adjustments

There are only three adjustments that can be made to emission carburetters in the field and these are:—

1. **Idling speed:** Ensure that the fast idle screw (1) (Fig. 3) is clear of the cam (2) and the choke lever is against its stop with the facia control pushed fully in. Unscrew the idling screw (3) until the throttle is just closed. Turn the screw 1½ turns to provide a datum setting.

   Start the engine and attain normal running temperature before final adjustment of the idling screw achieves a constant 800 to 850 rev/min.

2. **Fast idle speed setting:** Check that the mixture control cam lever (2) on both carburetters returns to its stop. Ensure that the mixture control cables are so adjusted that they are not slack or too tight. Pull the mixture control knob out on the facia and insert a 5/16 in (7.937 mm) diameter bar (5) between the cam and its stop on both carburetters in turn. Slacken the fast idle screw lock nut (1) on both carburetters and adjust the screws so that they just touch their respective cams. Remove the bar, push the control knob home and pull the control knob out again to check that the setting gives a fast idle speed of 1100 r.p.m. Make any necessary adjustments to the fast idle screw to achieve this setting whilst using the synchro check meter to maintain the carburetters in balance. Tighten the lock nuts, stop the engine, push the control knob fully home and refit the air cleaner.

   NOTE: If the engine is hot during the fast idle setting, the speed should be 1,500 rev/min.

3. **Idle emission:** An idle trimming screw (4) is provided to give very fine adjustment to compensate for the difference between a new 'stiff' engine and one that is 'run-in', THIS IS NOT AN ORDINARY MIXTURE ADJUSTING SCREW; it regulates a limited amount of air that can be introduced into the mixing chamber. It is important to remember that the ear will not detect any difference between the 'fully home' and 'fully open' position of the screw. The setting should therefore be checked by means of a CO meter or an air/fuel ratio meter to the exhaust pipe.

Carburetter Controls

The throttle rod linkage will not require adjustments during normal operation. To ensure complete throttle closure a degree of 'lost motion' or slackness is incorporated into the linkage; no attempt must be made to adjust this out.

Occasionally lubricate the linkage and choke cable with thin oil.

Carburetter Servicing Schedules

To maintain the carburetter at peak efficiency, regular servicing as detailed in the Maintenance Summary is essential. The appropriate servicing operations should be performed by authorized dealers, who are trained in the use of the special equipment needed. At 24,000 miles a carburetter overhaul using a special pack of gaskets, needle and needle valve will ensure that the emissions standards are upheld throughout the following maintenance period.

1. Pipe—crankcase breather
2. Pipe—Canister purge
3. Activated carbon canister
4. Pipe—Separator tank to canister
5. Fuel tank
6. Separator tank
7. Sealed filler cap
8. Run-on control valve

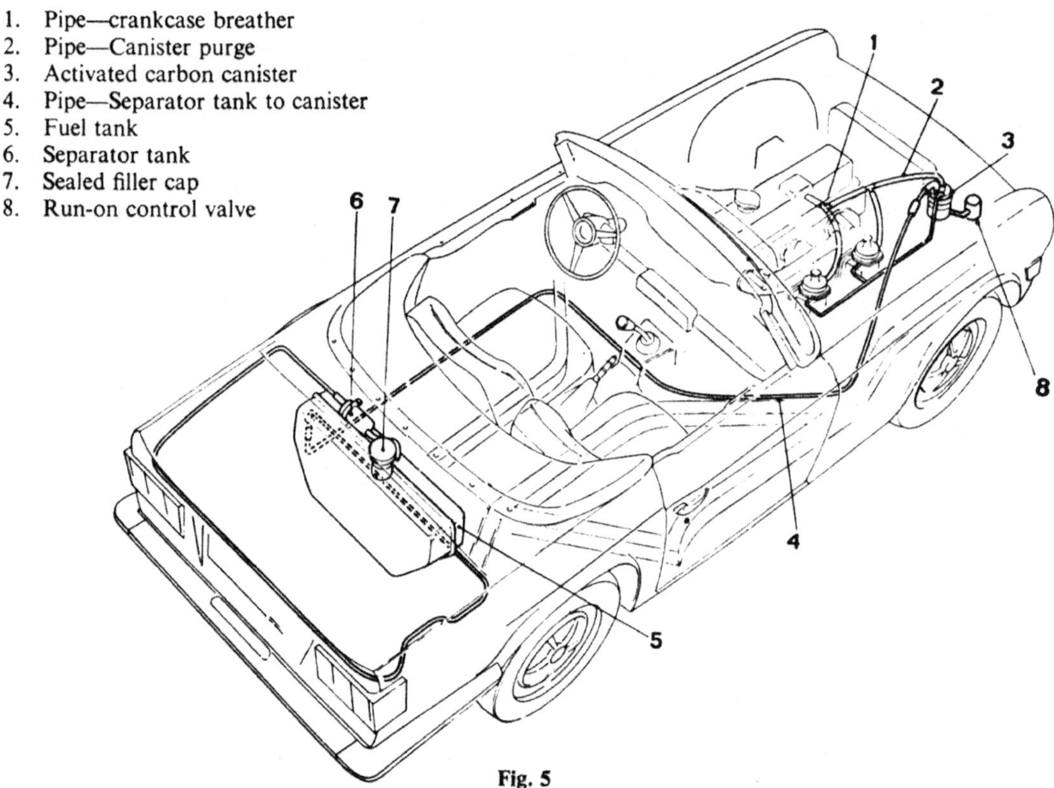

Fig. 5

Poor/rough idle	Loss of power/poor drive away	Misfiring (under load conditions)	High fuel consumption	High idling speed	Overheating (at idle speed)	Lean running	Arcing at plugs	Smell of fuel	Rich mixture	Stalling	Engine run on	Cause	Action
x	x	x										Distributor C.B. points	Check dwell angle/check gap and reset/renew points
x	x	x										Sparking plugs	Check gap and reset renew/defective plug
x	x	x					x					Ignition wiring	Inspect for fraying, chaffing and deterioration/renew
x	x		x									Choke mechanism	Check fast idle adjustment/cam and cable/adjust
x	x		x									Choke mechanism	Remove starter box and clean interface
x	x			x						x		Vacuum fittings, hoses and connections	Check piping condition and security/renew as necessary
x	x					x						Oil filler cap	Check for security/tighten cap
x	x					x						Ventilation hoses	Check hoses for security, blockage and deterioration
x			x									Carburetter	See carburetter fault finding chart
	x											Distributor	Lubricate/check operation by removing pipe and noting r.p.m.
	x		x									Carburetter air cleaner	Clean or renew element
			x	x								Ignition timing and advance systems	Check and reset dynamic timing
	(x)											Condensor and coil	Check for breakdown on oscillascope tune
			x					x				Hose connections	Check for hose damage and deterioration
									x			Carbon storage canister	Renew canister(s)
					(x)							Vacuum advance switch	Check switch operation and renew if necessary
											x	Run on valve	Check valve operation and renew if necessary

FAULT FINDING—EMISSION CARBURETTER

NOTE: Before undertaking extensive carburetter servicing it is recommended that other engine factors and components such as cylinder compressions, valve clearance, distributor, sparking plus, an intake temperature control system etc., are checked for correctness of operation.

SYMPTOM		CAUSE	ACTION
1. Poor idle quality.	a	Air leakage on indication manifold joints	Remake joints as necessary. Check idle carbon monoxide level with CO meter.
	b	Throttles not synchronized	Re-balance carburetters and reset linkage.
	c	Air valve or vales sticking in piston guide rods	Clean air valve rods and guides and reassemble. Check piston free movement by hand unit should move freely and return carburetter bridge with an audible click.
	d	Partially or fully obstructed float chamber or diaphragm ventilation holes	Check that gasket(s) are not causing obstruction or piping obstructed.
	e	Incorrect fuel level caused by maladjusted float assemblies or worn or dirty needle valve	Reset float heights and clean or replace needle valves worn.
	f	Metering needle incorrectly fitted or wrong type	Ensure shoulder of needle is flush with face of air valve and that needle bias is correct.
	g	Diaphragm incorrectly located or damaged	Check location with air valve cover removed, piston depression holes should be in line with and face towards the throttle spindle. Renew diaphragm with correct type if damage is in evidence.
	h	Leakage from retard pipe connections	Remake connections and recheck ignition settings.
	i	Temperature compensator faulty	With engine and carburetter cold check that compensator cone is seated and free to move off seat. If any doubt exists, replace unit with new assembly.
	j	After considerable service leakage may occur at throttle spindle or secondary throttle spindles.	Replace spindle seals or spindles as required.

SYMPTOM	CAUSE	ACTION
	Piston damper inoperative	Check damper oil level and top up with specified oil: recheck damper operation by raising piston by hand, whereupon resistence should be felt.
2. Hesitation or 'flat spot' a, b, c, d, e, f, g and h plus	Air valve spring missing or wrong part fitted	Check correct grade of spring and refit as required.
	Ignition timing incorrect	Check and reset as required.
	Throttle linkage operation incorrect	Check operation of linkage between carburetters and operation of secondary throttle links: reset or replace parts as required.
3. Heavy fuel consumption 1 and 2 plus	Leakage from the fuel connections, float chamber joints or sealing plug 'O' rings	Replace gaskets and 'O' rings as required.
	Faulty by-pass valve	Replace by-pass valve with new unit.
4. Lack of engine braking	Sticking throttles	Check throttle operation and reset as required.
	Ignition retard inoperative	Check ignition setting at idle and ensure correct functioning of retard system.
5. Lack of engine power	Damage diaphragm	Inspect and replace if incorrectly fitted or damaged.
	Low fuel flow	Check discharge from fuel pump. Inspect needle valve seating.

NOTE: To ensure compliance with exhaust emission legislative requirements for the following items MUST NOT be changed or modified in any way.

The fuel jet assembly; the air valve; the depression cover; the position of the fuel metering needle.

The following items must not be adjusted in service but should be replaced completely by factory-set units.

The temperature compensator; the air valve return spring; the by-pass unit; the starter assembly.

Engine—Daily

Prior to starting out on a long run, or every 250 miles (400 km.), check the engine oil level and, if necessary, add oil until the level reaches the high mark on the dipstick.

Before checking the level, make sure that the car is standing on level ground. The dipstick, located on the left-hand side of the crankcase (Fig. 1) may then be withdrawn, wiped clean and pushed fully home before withdrawing it for reading. Should the level be at the lower mark on the dipstick, 2·4 pints (U.S.A.) (1·14 litres) will be required for topping up via the cap (Fig. 2).

Brake Master Cylinder (1, Fig. 3)

Every week check the level of fluid in the brake master cylinder reservoir. The fluid level is visible through the translucent casing of the reservoir, **do not remove the cap.** A gradual lowering of the level over a long period is caused by brake pad wear and does not require topping-up. A sudden appreciable drop in the level must be investigated, the cause ascertained and rectified immediately.

Do not allow the level to drop below the danger line on the side of the casing.

To avoid dirt entering the system ensure that the reservoir is clean externally before removing the cap. Use only new fluid taken from a sealed container and re-seal the container after use. Replace the reservoir cap immediately after filling.

Radiator Water Level—Weekly (Fig. 2 page 26)

The level of water, visible through the translucent plastic reservoir mounted forward of the radiator, should be maintained at least "half-full" by adding soft water, when required, via the screwed cap.

Should the reservoir be allowed to empty, remove the radiator filler cap, completely fill the radiator, as described on page 25.

CAUTION: If the engine is hot, avoid danger from scalding by exercising extreme care when removing the radiator filler cap. Turn it a half-turn and allow pressure to be fully released before completely removing the cap.

Fig. 1   Fig. 2

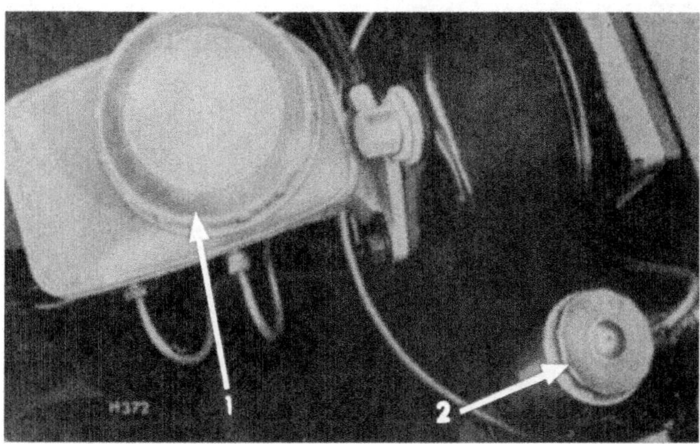

Fig. 3

Windshield Washer

Examine the water level in the plastic windshield washer container. If required, unscrew the cap and replenish the container with clean water. (Refer to page 26).

Battery—monthly

Examine the level of the electrolyte in the cells and, if necessary, add distilled water via the filler orifices to bring the level up to the top of the separators.

CAUTION: Never use a naked light when examining the battery. The mixture of oxygen and hydrogen given off by the battery is dangerously explosive.

Clutch Master Cylinder (2, Fig. 3).

Every month, check the level of fluid in the clutch master cylinder. To prevent dirt entering the system, clean the cap and surrounding area prior to removing the cap. Top-up the fluid until it is level with the line on the side of the reservoir.

1,000 MILES—FREE SERVICE

The engine oil pan is initially filled at the factory with a special running-in oil which should be drained after completing the first 1,000 miles (1,600 km.) and refilled with one of the high grade oils recommended. During this period many of the components, including the brakes, fan belt, gaskets, studs and nuts, settle down, thus necessitating slight adjustment and an overall check.

The owner is, therefore, urged at the completion of this period to return the vehicle to the selling dealer who will perform the operations recommended free-of-charge, except for oil and grease.

Fig. 4 (upper)   Fig. 5 (lower)

THE FOLLOWING OPERATIONS SHOULD BE CARRIED OUT AT THE INTERVALS RECOMMENDED IN THE MAINTENANCE SUMMARY

Engine Oil Pan (Fig. 4)

Remove the plug (arrowed), to drain the oil. Refit the plug and refill to the correct level, via the filler cap, (Fig. 2). Reduce this period according to the severity of the following unfavourable conditions.

1. Dusty roads.

2. Short journeys involving frequent stop/start driving, particularly during cold weather when greater use is made of the choke control.

If the vehicle is used for competition or sustained high speed work, the use of higher viscosity oil is recommended because of increased oil temperature.

Oil Filter Element (Fig. 5)

Unscrew the securing bolt (1), remove the container (2) and discard the element (3). Wash out the container and insert a new element.

Renew the sealing ring (4), ensuring that it is correctly located in the cylinder block and re-attach the filter assembly by tightening the bolt (1) sufficiently to ensure an oil-tight joint.

Air Cleaner (Figs. 6 and 7)

At the intervals stated in the "Passport to Service" or more frequently where conditions of extreme dust prevail, release the flexible hose (1) (early models only) from the plate (2). Unscrew six bolts (3) securing the container to the carburetor flanges, take off the cover plate (2) and lift out the elements (4), noting the positions of the rubber ring seals (5).

Clean out the container (6) and use a high pressure air line, or foot pump, to remove dust from between the folds of the paper element (4).

Re-assemble the air cleaner, ensuring that the slot (7) in the cover plate (2) and gasket (8) and the vent and bolt holes, align with those in the carburetor flanges.

Renew the paper elements at the intervals recommended in the "Passport to Service".

Compression Checks

Have the compression pressures checked by your Triumph Dealer. Providing that the engine is functioning satisfactorily, and the compression pressures of all the cylinders are equal, you are advised not to disturb the engine.

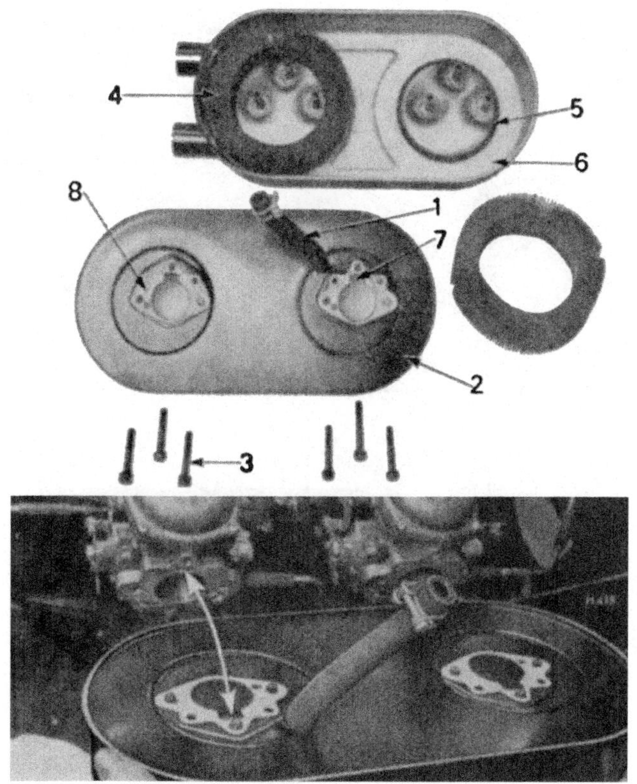

Fig. 6 (upper)   Fig. 7 (lower)

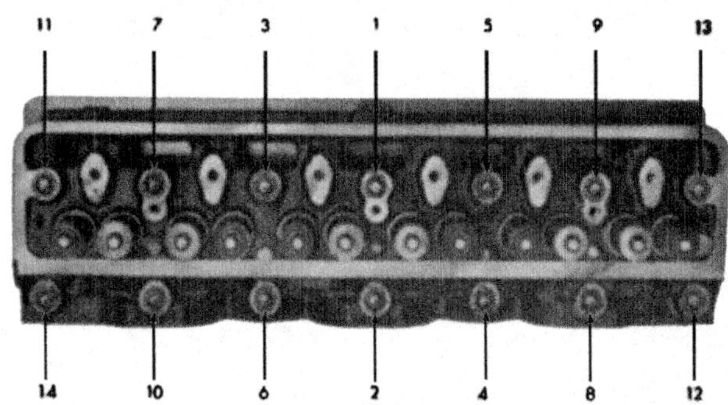

Fig. 8 (upper)   Fig. 9 lower)

The need for decarbonising arises when the build-up of carbon, a product of combustion, becomes excessive. If premium grade fuels and high quality lubricants are used, carbon deposit is so minimised that frequent decarbonising is unnecessary. Carbon removal may, therefore, be restricted to occasions when the cylinder head is removed for attention to the valves and seats.

Valve Clearances—Adjustment (Fig. 8)

Remove the rocker cover and, turning the engine clockwise, check and adjust the valve clearances to 0.010″ (0.25 mm.) if required, in the following sequence while the engine is cold:

Adjust Nos. 1 and 3 valves with Nos. 10 and 12 valves open

„   „   8 and 11 „   „   „   2 and 5 „   „

„   „   4 and 6 „   „   „   7 and 9 „   „

„   „   10 and 12 „   „   „   1 and 3 „   „

„   „   2 and 5 „   „   „   8 and 11 „   „

„   „   7 and 9 „   „   „   4 and 6 „   „

Refit the rocker cover.

Cylinder Head Nuts (Fig. 9)

When required, tighten the cylinder head nuts in the order shown. Slacken them by reversing the sequence.

Fuel Pump (Fig. 12)

Access to the petrol pump bowl and filter is gained by unscrewing the bolt (1) and removing the domed cover (2). Lift the filter gauze (3) from its seating and wash it in petrol.

Note: On later models a metal cover secured by one center screw replaces the translucent domed cover.

Using a small screwdriver, loosen the sediment in the bowl and blow it clear by using a jet of compressed air. A foot pump used for tyre inflation is ideal for this purpose.

Renew the cork gasket if it has hardened or is broken. Assemble the filter gauze (3) into its seating, taking care to place the gauze face downwards so that it can be removed easily when required.

Sparking Plugs

At the intervals recommended in the "Maintenance Summary".

(a) Remove sparking plugs for cleaning and reset the gaps to 0·25″ (0·63 mm.). Clean the ceramic insulators and examine them for cracks or other damage likely to cause "H.T." tracking. Test the plugs and renew those which are suspect.

or (b) Renew all the sparking plugs. Ensure that they are of the correct type (page 66) and that the gaps are set to 0·25″ (0·63 mm.).

Replace plug leads in the order shown in Fig. 11, i.e. firing order 1, 5, 3, 6, 2, 4.

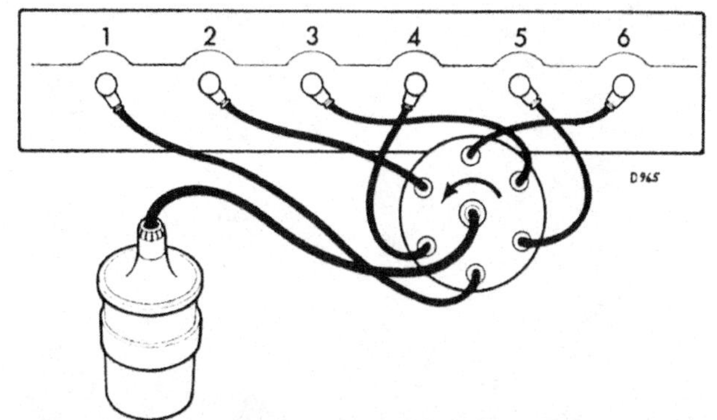

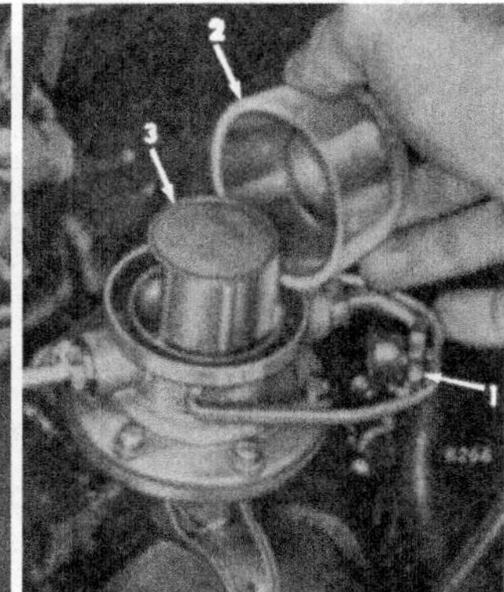

Fig. 10 (left)   **Fig. 11 (upper)**   **Fig. 12 (right)**

Fuel Filter (Fig. 10)

Renew the filter, ensure that the new filter is fitted according to the direction of flow as stated on the filter casing.

Carbon Canister (Fig, 1 page 43)

Remove the carbon canister as follows:—disconnect the three pipes from the top of the canister and the connection to the running on control valve from the bottom. Remove the nut and bolt on the securing strap and lift out the canister. When fitting a new canister ensure that all connections are leak free and that no pipes are kinked.

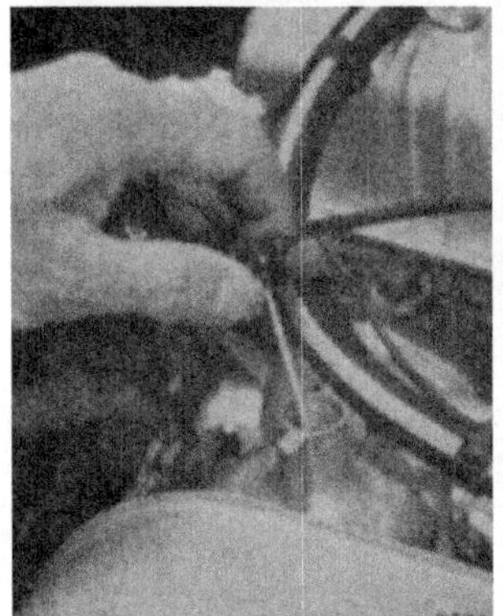

Engine Breather Pipes (Fig. 1 Page 43)

Remove and clean the piping connecting the rocker cover to the carburetors and the carbon canister. Clean breather oil filter or rocker cover filter in clean fuel.

Ignition Distributor (Fig. 14)

Release the clips and remove the distributor cap and rotor arm. Smear the cam (4) lightly with oil and apply a few drops of thin oil to the screw (1), in the center of the cam, and a single drop on the contact breaker pivot (2).

Fig. 13 (left)   **Fig. 14 (upper)**   **Fig. 15 (right)**

Turn the engine until the contact breaker lever (3) is operating on the highest point of the cam lobe, i.e. gap at its widest. Slacken the fixed contact screw (5), insert a screwdriver into the "Vee"-shaped cut-out (7) in the contact lever (6) and adjust the lever to obtain 0·015″ (0·4 mm.) gap using a feeler gauge between the contacts and retighten screw (2). Refit the rotor arm and cap.

Renew worn or damaged points when required.

Note: On later models the distributor may have only one vacuum connection. However, the above instructions for adjustment apply to either type of distributor.

Carburetor Dampers (Fig. 13)

Unscrew and withdraw the plug and damper assembly from the top of each carburetor. Top-up the damper chambers with the seasonal grade of engine oil. The oil level is correct when utilising the damper as a dipstick its threaded plug is ¼″ (6 mm.) above the dash pots, when resistance is felt. Refit the damper.

Using an oil can, apply oil to the throttle and choke control linkages.

Fan Belt Adjustment (Fig. 15)

Slacken the pivot bolt nut (1) and the adjustment bracket bolt (2). Pivot the alternator away from the engine until the belt can be moved ¾″—1″ (19—25 mm.) at the mid-point of its longest run. Maintaining the alternator in this position, tighten the bolt (2) and nut (1).

Transmission (Fig. 16)

With the vehicle standing on level ground, remove the oil filler plug (shown arrowed), and top up the transmission until

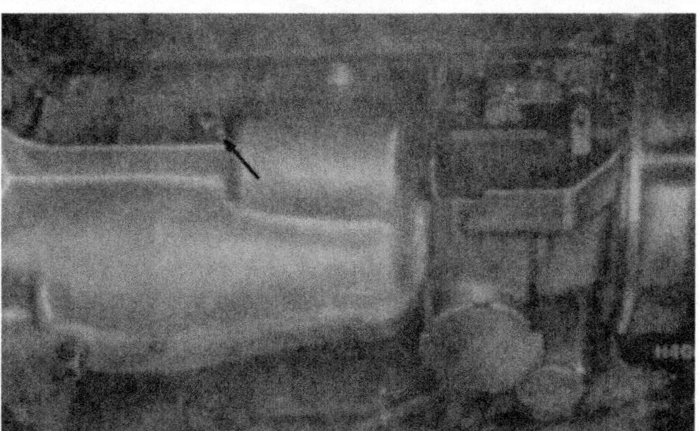

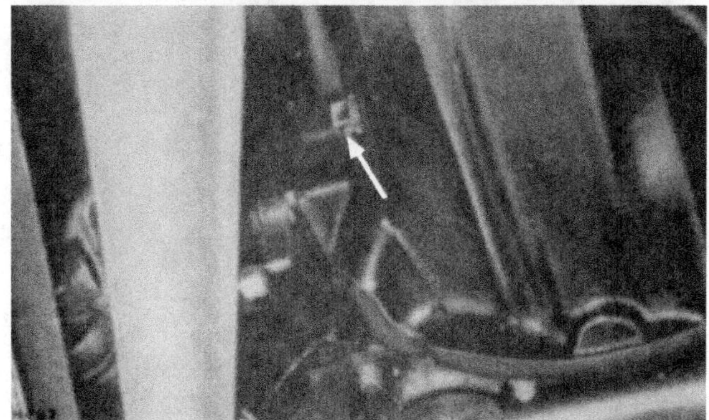

Fig. 16 (upper)   Fig. 17 (lower)

the oil is level with the bottom of the filler plug threads. Allow surplus oil to drain away before refitting the plug and wiping clean. An oil transfer hole between the transmission and overdrive unit provides a common oil level. Maintenance of the overdrive unit is thus limited to ensuring that the correct oil level is maintained in the gearbox.

Final Drive (Fig. 17)

Remove the oil level plug (shown arrowed), and top-up the rear axle until the oil is level with the bottom of the filler plug threads. Allow surplus oil to drain before refitting the plug and wiping clean.

Propellor Shaft (Fig. 18)

Check the coupling bolts for tightness.

Water Pump (Fig. 19)

Remove the sealing plug (if fitted) from the water pump and replace it by a grease nipple ($\frac{1}{8}''$ Briggs taper). Apply a grease gun until grease exudes from a pressure release hole in the side of the water pump. Replace the sealing plug.

Where no sealing plug is fitted—lubrication is not necessary.

Inner Drive Shafts (Fig. 20)

Apply a grease gun filled with grease to the nipple (arrowed) and give 5 strokes only.

Check the coupling bolts for tightness.

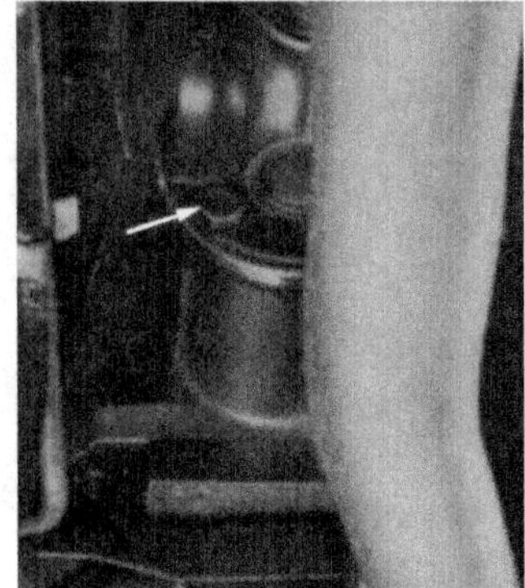

Fig. 18 (left)　　　Fig. 19 (upper)　　　Fig. 20 (right)

Steering Unit (Fig. 22)

Remove a sealing plug from the top of the steering unit and replace it by a grease nipple ($\frac{1}{8}''$ B.S.P. Parallel). Apply the grease gun and give 5 strokes only. Remove the nipple and refit the plug.

Lower Steering Swivel (Fig. 23)

Remove the plug (arrowed) and fit a suitable nipple. Fit a grease gun charged with oil and stroke until *oil* exudes from the swivel. Remove the nipple and refit the plug.

Upper Ball Joint (Fig. 21)

Apply a grease fun filled with grease to the nipple (arrowed). Pump the gun until grease exudes from the underside of the nylon washer retained by the grease nipple.

Tightness Check

Check and if necessary, tighten the steering unit attachments and "U" bolts, steering tie rods and levers.

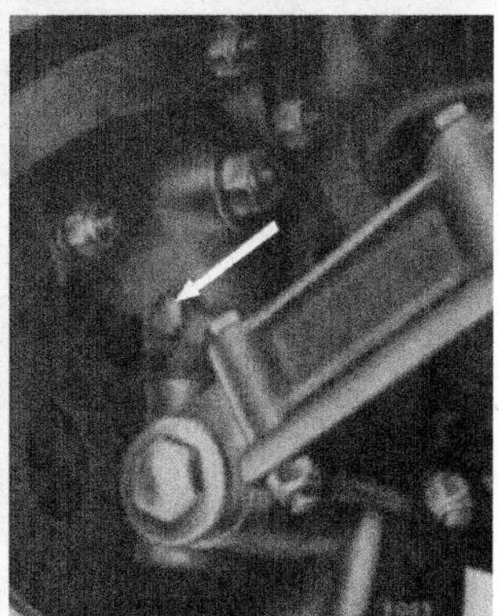

Fig. 21 (left)   **Fig. 22 (upper)**   **Fig. 23 (right)**

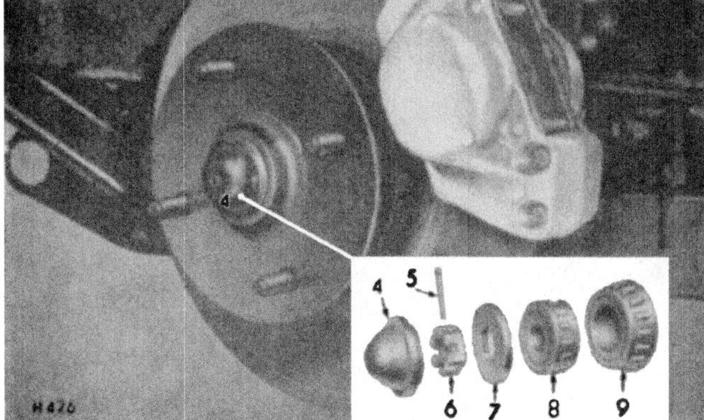

Fig. 24 (upper)   Fig. 25 (lower)

Front Hub Adjustment and Lubrication (Figs. 24 and 25)

Check and if necessary adjust the front hubs.

At major overhaul periods, re-pack the front hubs with grease.

Jack up the front of the car and remove one front road wheel. Unscrew two bolts (1) securing the caliper (2) to the disc mounting plate (3).

Lift the caliper from the disc tying it to a convenient point to prevent it hanging by the attached hydraulic pipe. Note the number of shims fitted between the caliper and the vertical link.

When wire-spoked wheels are fitted, remove the splined hub extensions by detaching the nuts.

Remove the hub grease cap (4), withdraw the split pin (5) and remove the slotted nut (6) and "D" washer (7). Detach the hub assembly from the stub axle. Remove outer (8) and inner (9) race from the hub (inset Fig. 25). Wash all trace of grease from the hub bearings. Pack the hub bearings with new grease, working it well into the rollers.

Re-assemble the hub and races to the stub axle, securing them with the "D" washer and slotted nut. Spin the hub and tighten the nut until resistance is felt to hub rotation, then slacken off the nut one half flat and fit a new split pin. Re-assemble the brake caliper unit to the vertical link, refitting any shims removed during dismantling. Re-assemble the splined hub extension (if fitted). Refit the road wheel and lower the jack.

Repeat the above operations with the opposite wheel hub.

Exhaust System

Check the complete exhaust system for leaks and immediately rectify defects.

Wheel Alignment

Check the front and rear wheel track alignment if tire wear is uneven. See page 22.

Electrical

Check the operation of all electrical equipment and adjust, if necessary, the headlight settings.

Brakes

The brakes are hydraulically operated and vacuum-servo assisted. Self-adjusting disc brakes are fitted to the front; leading and trailing shoe drum brakes are fitted at the rear of the car. The handbrake lever is connected to the rear brakes only, by twin cables.

At the Intervals Recommended in the "Maintenance Summary"

(a) Check and adjust the brakes as necessary.

(b) Chock the front wheels, jack up the rear of the car and remove both road wheels and brake drums. Examine the brake linings for wear and freedom from oil or grease. Renew worn or contaminated linings.

Using compressed air, blow all dust from the mechanism and, using a dry clean cloth, wipe the dust from the inside of the drums. Avoid touching the braking surfaces with greasy hands.

Refit the brake drums and road wheels, re-adjust the brakes and remove the jack.

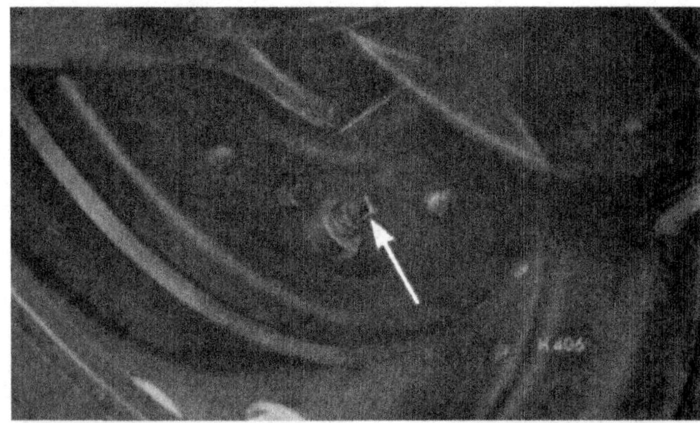

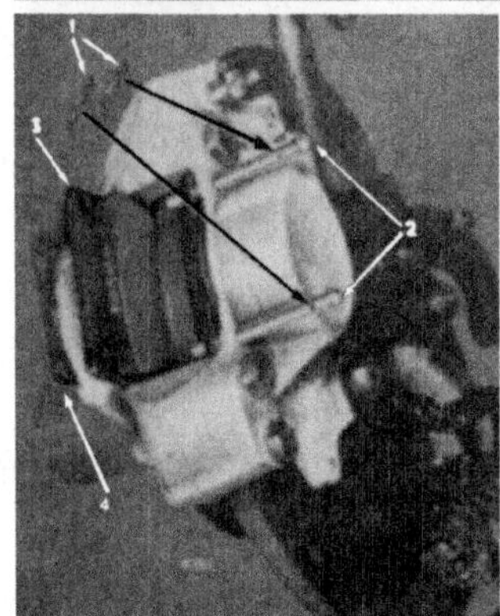

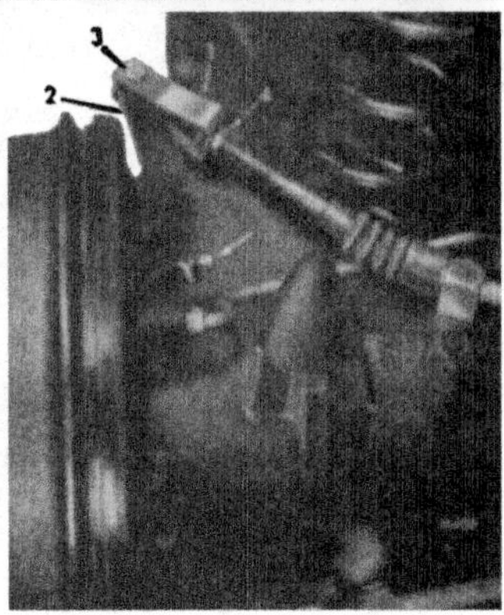

Fig. 26 (left)   Fig. 27 (upper)   Fig. 28 (right)

Front Brakes—Renewing Friction Pads (Fig. 26)

When friction pads are reduced to $\frac{1}{8}''$ (3 mm.) thickness, or if they are of insufficient thickness to ensure safe braking for a further 6,000 miles (10,000 km.) renew them as follows:

1. Apply the handbrake, jack up the front of the car and remove the front road wheels.

2. Release the retaining clips (1) and remove the pad retaining pins (2).

3. Lift the friction pads (3) and the anti-squeal plates (4) from the caliper.

IMPORTANT. Do not depress the brake pedal with the pads removed.

4. Clean the exposed faces of the pistons and the recesses into which the pads fit, then carefully push the pistons back into the calipers.

NOTE. This action will displace fluid back into the master cylinder reservoir. To prevent over-flowing, syphon off surplus fluid.

5. Fit the brake pads and anti-squeal plates, ensuring that the arrows on the plates are pointing in the direction of wheel rotation.

6. Insert the pad retaining pins and secure them with the spring clips.

7. Pump the brake pedal several times to adjust the brakes and check the level of fluid in the reservoir.

8. Replace the front wheels and remove the jack.

Rear Brakes—Adjusting (Fig. 27)

Each rear brake is provided with an adjuster which is accessible when the rear road wheel is removed. To adjust the shoes, let the parking brake off, turn the adjuster clockwise until the shoes are hard against the drum, then slacken the adjuster by one notch increments until the drum is free to rotate.

Parking Brake—Adjusting (Fig. 28)

The parking brake is automatically adjusted when the rear drum brakes are adjusted; however, remove slackness, accruing in the cables by the following procedure:

1. Release the parking brake lever, chock the front wheels, jack up the rear of the car and remove the rear road wheels.

2. Detach the fork end (1) from the lever (2) by removing the clevis pin (3) which is secured by a split pin.

3. Adjust the brake shoes hard against the drum.

4. Slacken the locknut (4) and turn the fork end clockwise to reduce the effective length of the cable.

5. Adjust both cables equally until the clevis pins can be inserted without tension on the brake cables or the backplate levers.

6. Slacken the adjuster until the drums are free to rotate.

7. Tighten the locknut and replace the fork-end, clevis pin, and washer and fit a new split pin. Apply a little grease around the fork ends, replace wheels and remove the jack.

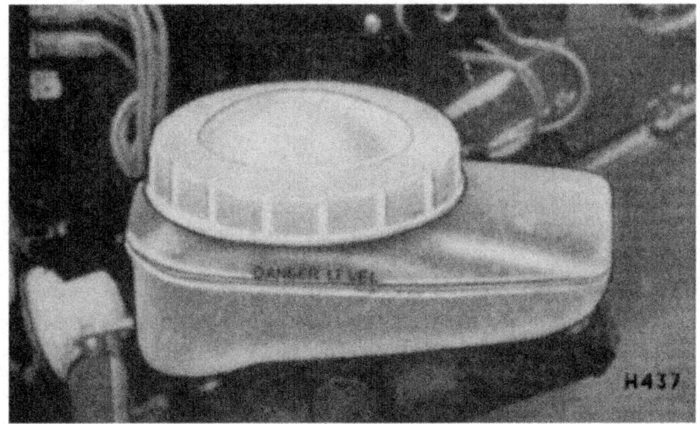

Fig. 29

Vacuum Servo Unit

The TR6 is fitted with a brake servo unit, which, utilising engine manifold depression multiplies the effort applied to the brake pedal.

The servo unit is in direct line between the pedal and the master cylinder. The system is arranged so that if, for any reason, the servo system is inoperative braking can still be effected, though requiring greatly increased pedal effort.

CAUTION: For reasons given above, it is extremely dangerous to "coast" or manoeuvre the car without the engine running.

HYDRAULIC SYSTEM

Description

The foot operated hydraulic braking system employs a tandem master cylinder for transmitting pressure to independent front and rear braking systems. Both systems are connected to opposing sides of a pressure differential warning actuator (P.D.W.A.) which operates an electrical switch when a pressure drop on one side of the valve causes a shuttle to move from its mid-position. The P.D.W.A. switch operates a warning light on the facia (Fig. 2 page 6) which is series/parallel connected with the oil warning light. Thus when the brakes are working correctly, the brake warning light and the oil warning light are both extinguished as the engine speed is increased from idle (giving regular assurance that the brake warning light is functioning). In the event of a partial brake failure the brake warning system is earthed directly, causing the warning light to glow brightly.

Bleeding the Hydraulic Braking System
General

If air has entered either of the hydraulic braking systems then only the system affected need be bled. During bleeding, exercise care, as described in the following procedure, to avoid moving the shuttle from its mid-position. However, if the shuttle has moved during bleeding or subsequent to a fault condition, centralise the shuttle by performing operations 5—9 opposite.

Preparation for Bleeding

Before commencing to bleed the brakes ensure that all the bleed nipples (Figs. 26 and 28) are clean and, taking care to avoid dirt entering the fluid reservoir, remove its filler cap and top-up with new hydraulic fluid. During the bleeding operation keep the level of the fluid above the dividing partition in the reservoir. Do not use fluid bled from the system for topping-up.

Use new fluid from a sealed container, resealing the container after use.

Procedure

Commence with the brake, of the pair being bled, farthest from the master cylinder. If both systems are to be bled, bleed the rear brakes first. When bleeding the rear brakes, release the handbrake and turn the brake adjusters to lock the shoes against the drums. When bleeding is completed adjust the brakes as detailed on page 65.

1. Attach a rubber tube of approx. $\frac{1}{4}''$ (6 mm.) bore to the brake bleed nipple allowing the other end of the tube to hang submerged in a jar containing a quantity of clean brake fluid.

2. Unscrew the bleed-screw enough to allow the fluid to be pumped out (half a turn is normally sufficient).

3. Depress the brake pedal and allow it to return slowly noting that only a LIGHT pedal effort is required and the pedal must NOT be pushed through at the end of the stroke. (In addition, never "try" the pedal until all air has been dispelled and the system is fully bled, as either action will cause the shuttle to move and actuate the switch). Pausing between each depression of the pedal, continue pumping until all air has been dispelled from the bleed-screw (denoted by the absence of bubbles in the fluid being pumped into the jar).

4. With the pedal depressed, close the bleed-screw nipple and repeat the operation on the other brake.

Procedure for Re-centralising the P.D.W.A. Piston

If, for reasons described above, the P.D.W.A. shuttle requires to be re-centralised, adopt the following procedure.

5. Fit a rubber tube, as described in 1 above, to a brake bleed-screw at the opposite end of the car to that which has just been bled.

6. Open the bleed-screw.

7. Switch the ignition on but DO NOT START THE ENGINE. (The brake warning light will glow but the oil warning light will remain extinguished).

8. Exert a steady pressure on the brake pedal until the brake light dims and the oil light glows. (A click should be felt on the pedal as the shuttle returns to its mid-position).

9. Tighten the bleed-screw.

NOTE: If the pedal has been pushed too hard the shuttle will move to the other side of the valve, thus requiring the procedure to be repeated on a brake at the opposite end of the car.

Clutch and Brake Pipe Hoses

Examine and renew defective hoses. Ensure that pipes and hoses have adequate clearance to prevent chafing against other components, particularly when the steering is turned to "full lock" in either direction.

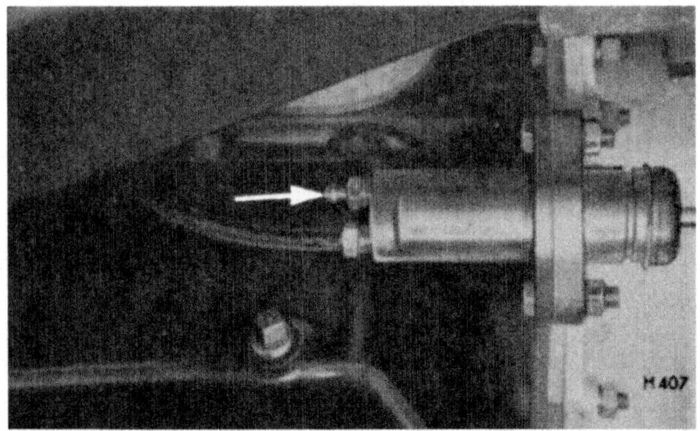

Fig. 30

Bleeding the Clutch System (Fig. 3 page 51 and Fig. 30 page 66)

When a pipe joint has been disconnected, or part of the hydraulic clutch system dismantled, bleed all air from the system as follows:

1. Clean the neck and cap of the master cylinder (2. Fig. 3 page 51).

2. Remove the cap and top-up with new hydraulic fluid. (At no time, during the subsequent operation, allow the level of fluid to fall below half full.)

3. Clean the clutch cylinder nipple (Fig. 30) and attach to it a rubber tube of approx. $\frac{1}{4}''$ (6 mm.) bore allowing the other end of the tube to hang submerged in a jar containing a quantity of clean hydraulic fluid.

4. Unscrew the bleed nipple enough to allow fluid to be pumped out (a half turn is normally sufficient).

5. Depress the clutch pedal firmly and allow it to return unassisted. Pausing between each depression continue pumping until all air has been expelled from the system (denoted by the absence of bubbles in the fluid being pumped into the jar).

6. With the pedal depressed, close the bleed nipple.

(The products recommended are not listed in order of preference)

<table>
<tr>
<td rowspan="2">COMPONENT</td>
<td colspan="2">Air temp.</td>
<td rowspan="2">API Desig-nation</td>
<td rowspan="2">BP</td>
<td rowspan="2">CASTROL</td>
<td rowspan="2">DUCK-HAMS</td>
<td rowspan="2"></td>
<td rowspan="2">ESSO</td>
<td rowspan="2"></td>
<td rowspan="2">MOBIL</td>
<td rowspan="2">PETRO-FINA</td>
<td rowspan="2">SHELL</td>
<td rowspan="2">TEXACO</td>
</tr>
<tr>
<td>°C</td>
<td>°F</td>
</tr>
<tr>
<td>** ENGINE</td>
<td>over 30</td>
<td>over 80</td>
<td>SD</td>
<td rowspan="4">* BP Super Visco-Static</td>
<td rowspan="2">Castrol GTX of Castrol XLR</td>
<td>Q20-50</td>
<td rowspan="3">Q 0--50</td>
<td rowspan="2">Esso Extra Motor Oil 20W/50</td>
<td rowspan="3">UNIFLO</td>
<td rowspan="2">Mobiloil Super 10W/50 Mobiloil Special 20W/50</td>
<td rowspan="2">Fina Supergrade Motor Oil 20W/50</td>
<td rowspan="2">Shell Super Motor Oil 100 20W/50</td>
<td rowspan="2">Havoline 20W/50</td>
</tr>
<tr>
<td>CARBURETTER DASHPOTS</td>
<td>30 to 0</td>
<td>80 to 30</td>
<td>SD</td>
<td></td>
</tr>
<tr>
<td>OIL-CAN</td>
<td>0 to −20</td>
<td>30 to −4</td>
<td>SD</td>
<td>Castrolite</td>
<td>Q5500</td>
<td>Esso Extra Motor Oil 10W/30</td>
<td>Mobiloil Super 10W/50</td>
<td>Fina Supergrade Motor Oil 10W/30</td>
<td>Shell Super Motor Oil 10W/30</td>
<td>Havoline 10W/30</td>
</tr>
<tr>
<td></td>
<td>below −20</td>
<td>below −4</td>
<td>SD</td>
<td>Castrol 5W/20</td>
<td>Q5W/30</td>
<td></td>
<td>Esso Extra Motor Oil 5W/20</td>
<td></td>
<td>Mobiloil 5W/20</td>
<td>Fina Supergrade 5W/20</td>
<td>Shell Winter Oil 5W/20</td>
<td>Havoline 5W/20</td>
</tr>
<tr>
<td rowspan="2">GEARBOX OVERDRIVE REAR AXLE, AND LOWER STEERING SWIVELS</td>
<td>over 0</td>
<td>over 30</td>
<td>GL4</td>
<td>BP Gear Oil SAE 90 EP</td>
<td>Castrol Hypoy</td>
<td>Duckhams Hypoid 90</td>
<td></td>
<td>Esso Gear Oil GX 90</td>
<td></td>
<td>Mobilube GX 90</td>
<td>Fina Pontonic MP SAE 90</td>
<td>Shell Spirax 90 EP</td>
<td>Multigear Lubricant EP 90</td>
</tr>
<tr>
<td>below 0</td>
<td>below 30</td>
<td>GL4</td>
<td>BP Gear Oil SAE 80 EP</td>
<td>Castrol Hypoy 80</td>
<td>Duckhams Hypoid 80</td>
<td></td>
<td>Esso Gear Oil GX 80</td>
<td></td>
<td>Mobilube GX 80</td>
<td>Fina Pontonic MP SAE 80</td>
<td>Shell Spirax 80 EP</td>
<td>Multigear Lubricant EP 80</td>
</tr>
<tr>
<td colspan="4">FRONT AND REAR HUBS BRAKE CABLES GREASE GUN</td>
<td>BP Energrease L2</td>
<td>Castrol LM Grease</td>
<td>Duckhams LB 10</td>
<td></td>
<td>Esso Multi-purpose Grease H</td>
<td></td>
<td>Mobilgrease MP</td>
<td>Fina Marson HTL 2</td>
<td>Shell Retinax A</td>
<td>Marfax All-purpose</td>
</tr>
<tr>
<td colspan="14">* Oils marked thus are available in Multigrade forms with viscosity characteristics appropriate to the ambient temperature in individual markets
** Where circuit racing or other severe competitive events are contemplated it is advisable, in view of the increased oil temperature encountered, to use oils of high viscosity</td>
</tr>
<tr>
<td colspan="4">CLUTCH AND BRAKE RESERVOIRS</td>
<td colspan="10">CASTROL GIRLING BRAKE AND CLUTCH FLUID CRIMSON, WHERE THIS PROPRIETARY BRAND IS NOT AVAILABLE, OTHER FLUIDS WHICH MEET SAE 71703 SPECIFICATION MAY BE USED</td>
</tr>
<tr>
<td colspan="4" rowspan="2">APPROVED ANTI-FREEZE SOLUTIONS</td>
<td>Smiths Bluecol</td>
<td>BP Anti-Freeze</td>
<td>Castrol Anti-Freeze</td>
<td colspan="2">Duckhams Anti-Freeze</td>
<td colspan="2">Esso Anti-Freeze</td>
<td>Mobil Permazone</td>
<td>Fina Thermidor</td>
<td>Shell Anti-Freeze</td>
<td>Startex</td>
</tr>
<tr>
<td colspan="10">Where these proprietary solutions are not available, others which meet BSI 3151 or 3152 specification may be used</td>
</tr>
</table>

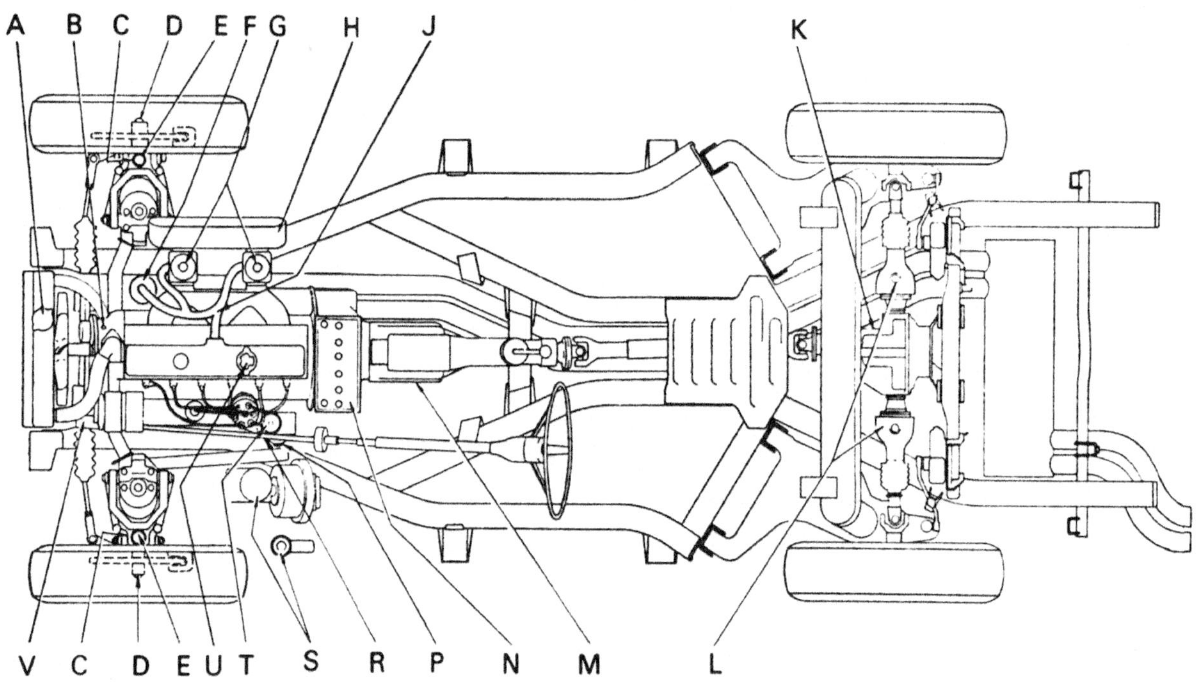

Fig. 31

Chart Ref.	Items	Details	Page Ref.	
A	Radiator	Top up	45	Weekly
B	Water Pump	Grease	54	———
C	Upper Ball Joints	Grease	55	———
D	Front Hubs	Adjust	56	———
E	Lower Steering Swivels	Grease	55	———
F	Evaporation Canister	Renew element	52	
F	Evaporation Canister	Renew canister	52	48,000 miles
G	Carburetor Dampers	Top up	53	———
H	Air Cleaners	Clean	49	———
H	Air Cleaners	Renew element	49	———
J	Breather Piping	Clean	52	
K	Final Drive	Top up	54	———
L	Drive Shafts	Grease	54	———
M	Gearbox	Top up	53	———
N	Battery	Top up	46	Monthly
P	Oil Filter	Renew element	48	———
R	Fuel Filter	Renew	51	———
S	Master Cylinder—Brake Master Cylinder—Clutch	Check	45	Weekly
S	Master Cylinder—Brake Master Cylinder—Clutch	Top up	46	Monthly
T	Fuel Pump	Clean	51	———
U	Engine Oil Pan	Top up	45	Daily
U	Engine Oil Pan	Drain and refill	48	———
V	Steering Unit	Grease	55	———

FOR MAINTENANCE PERIODS REFER TO THE MAINTENANCE SUMMARY

GENERAL SPECIFICATION

Engine

Number of cylinders	6	
Bore of cylinders	74·7 mm.	2·94 in.
Stroke of crankshaft	95 mm.	3·74 in.
Cubic capacity	2498 c.c.	152 in.^{3}
Piston area	263 cm.^{2}	40·7 in.^{2}
Compression ratio	7·75 : 1	
Valve rocker clearances (cold)	0·25 mm.	0·010 in.
Valve timing	Inlet and exhaust equally open at T.D.C.	

Lubrication (Engine)

Pump	High capacity eccentric lobe type
Filter	Full flow type, replaceable element

Cooling System

	Pressurised "no loss" system incorporating a translucent plastic overflow bottle
Circulation	"Vee" belt driven pump
Fan	13 blades, 14·5 in. dia. (36·8 cm.)

Fuel System

Pump	A.C. mechanically operated diaphragm type
Carburetor	Twin sidedraught Stromberg 175 C.D.S.E.V.
Manifolds	Cast aluminium inlet manifold and cast iron outlet exhaust manifold
Air cleaners	Replaceable paper elements
Crankcase breathing	Closed circuit breathing from rocker cover to constant depression area of carburetors

Ignition System

Coil	Lucas HA12
Distributor—type	Lucas with centrifugal advance and vacuum retard
contact gap	0·015 in. (0·4 mm.)
rotation—viewed on rotor	Anticlockwise
Firing order	1 - 5 - 3 - 6 - 2 - 4
Sparking plugs—type	Champion UN—12Y
gap	0·025 in. (0·63 mm.)
Ignition timing (static)	12 degrees B.T.D.C.
Ignition timing (idle)	4 degrees A.T.D.C.

Electrical System

Voltage	12
Polarity	Negative earth
Fuses—fuse box	35 amp.
Alternator—type	Lucas 17ACR—with integral control unit
—nominal output	36 amps.
Battery—type	Lucas
—capacity @ 20 hour rate	57 amp. hour
—plates per cell	9
—normal charge rate	5 amps.
Starter motor	Lucas M100 pre-engaged type
Turn signal flasher unit	Lucas 8FL 3·6A
Hazard flasher unit	Lucas 9FL 10A max
Fuel and temperature indication	Smiths bi-metal resistance 10 volt system
Oil pressure indication- switch operating pressure	3–5 lb. in.^{2} (0·2–0·35 kg/cm.^{2})

Transmission

Clutch — Diaphragm type 8½ in. dia. (21·5 cms.)

Transmission — Four forward ratios and one reverse Synchromesh on all forward ratios Overdrive available as optional equipment: Ratio 0·82 : 1

	O/D Top	Top	3rd	O/D 3rd	2nd	1st	Rev.
Ratios	0·797	1·00	1·06	1·33	2·01	3·14	3·22
Overall ratios	2·95	3·70	3·92	4·92	7·44	11·62	11·9

Rear axle — Semi-floating axle shafts, three-piece casing. Hypoid bevel gears 3·7 : 1 ratio

Wheels — Steel disc type. Rim section 5½J.

Tires — Refer to page 22

Brake System — Girling tandem hydraulic system incorporating direct acting servo unit

Front	Caliper disc 10⅞ in. dia. (27·62 cms.)	
Rear	Drums 9 in. dia. (22·9 cms.) 1¾ in. (4·45 cms.)	
Front lining area	20·7 in.²	133·6 cms.²
Front swept area	233 in.²	1483·8 cms.²
Rear lining area	60·5 in.²	390·0 cms.²
Rear swept area	99 in.²	638·7 cms.²
Total lining area	81·2 in.²	522·8 cms.²
Total swept area	332 in.²	2139 cms.²
Maximum retardation	·98 G	

Suspension

Front	Low periodicity independent system. Patented bottom bush and top ball joint wheel swivels. Coil springs controlled by telescopic dampers. Taper roller hub bearings.
Rear	Semi-trailing arm independent suspension with coil springs controlled by piston dampers. Mounted on frame through rubber bushed pivots and with rubber insulation of the spring.

Chassis Data

Frame	Channel steel pressing of box section side members braced by a cruciform member	
Wheelbase	7 ft. 4 in.	2240 mm.
Track—Front	4 ft. 2¼ in.	1276 mm.
—Rear	4 ft. 1¾ in.	1264 mm.
Ground clearance	6 in.	152 mm.
Turning circle	34 ft.	10·4 m.
Steering unit	Rack and pinion 3¼ turns lock to lock	

Capacities	Imperial	Metric	U.S.A.
Fuel tank	9½ galls.	43·0 litres	11·4 galls.
Engine sump	9 pints	5·11 litres	10·8 pints
Gearbox from dry	2 pints	1·13 litres	2·4 pints
Gearbox and overdrive	2·66 pints	1·5 litres	3·2 pints
Rear axle from dry	2¼ pints	1·42 litres	2·7 pints
Cooling system (inc. water bottle) with heater	11 pints	6·2 litres	13·2 pints

Exterior Dimensions

Overall length	12 ft. 11 in.	3937 mm.
Width	4 ft. 10 in.	1470 mm.
Height with hood erected (unladen)	4 ft. 2 in.	1270 mm.
Height with hood folded (unladen)	3 ft. 10 in.	1170 mm.

Weight (approx.)

Dry (excluding extra equipment)	2280 lbs.	1034 kg.
Complete (including fuel, oil, water and tools)	2390 lbs.	1084 kg.
Maximum gross vehicle weight	2960 lbs.	1342 kg.
Vehicle capacity weight	412 lbs.	187 kg.

Road Speed Data

Engine speed at a road speed of:	O/D Top	O/D Top	3rd	3rd	2nd	1st
10 m.p.h.	383	482	510	641	969	1513
10 k.p.h.	240	300	319	398	602	940

Road speed at 1,000 r.p.m. in top gear	20.74 m.p.h.	33.4 k.p.h.
O/D Top	26.1 m.p.h.	42.0 k.p.h.
Road speed at 2,500 ft./min. piston speed in top gear	83 m.p.h.	134 k.p.h.

Emission Control System Warranty

for 1973 models

British Leyland Motors Inc.
600 Willow Tree Road, Leonia, New Jersey 07605

British Leyland Motors Inc., 600 Willow Tree Road, Leonia, New Jersey 07605, warrants to the ultimate purchaser and each subsequent purchaser of the vehicle that it has been designed, built and equipped so as to conform at the time of sale with all U.S. emission standards applicable at the time of manufacture, and that it is free from defects in materials and workmanship which would cause it not to meet these standards for five years from the first retail delivery of the vehicle or 50,000 miles, whichever occurs first. Failures which result from lack of proper maintenance or from misuse or abuse of the vehicle or engine are not covered by this Warranty.

Like any other piece of complicated machinery, your car will need regular attention and service to make sure that the Emission Control System continues to function properly. This is the owner's responsibility. The manufacturer cannot guarantee that emissions will not rise to unacceptable levels if maintenance of the System is not carefully and regularly done as provided in this manual.

The warranty guarantees the Emission Control System to be free of "defects". Ordinary wear and tear on the vehicle and the engine, sufficient to require replacement of parts and components at regular intervals, is not evidence of a "defect." As these may affect performance of the Emission Control System, the owner should have these regularly inspected during the Recommended Service Procedures, and replaced where necessary. Some of these replacement items (such as spark plugs) are scheduled for regular replacement under the Maintenance Guide-lines. Other illustrations: mufflers and other parts of the exhaust system will normally require replacement during five years; engine valves must be regularly inspected, and replaced where necessary, in order to make sure that emissions will not rise to unacceptable levels. No condition is regarded as a "defect" if it results from a failure to follow recommended service instructions, including component replacement as indicated.

Failure of the System may also result from misuse or abuse of the car or its engine. Operation of the car at excessive speeds, or overloaded, or under heavy dust condition, may adversely affect the functioning of the Emission Control System. So may racing the car, or fire or accident caused to the car. If the car is operated only on short trips, or is not, generally speaking, driven each day for at least several miles, some components of the Emission Control System may deteriorate more rapidly than would otherwise be expected, and this does not show a "defect".

Use of Unleaded Fuels. Regular use of unleaded or low-lead gasolines may cause difficulties with the engine and will result in malfunctions of the Emission Control System. The anti-wear additives found in leaded gasolines are necessary to avoid difficulties of this type. While an occasional tankful of unleaded or low-lead fuel is unlikely to cause such problems, conditions attributable to sustained use of such fuels will not be considered "defects".

These examples are given to show the limits on the manufacturer's responsibility under the Emission Control System Warranty. As in the case of other non-warranty work, the owner will be charged by the dealer for labor, parts and lubricants. We are sure you will find this money well spent as your contribution to cleaner air and an improved environment.

INDEX

Brooklands Books Ltd., P.O. Box 904, Amersham, Bucks., HP6 9JA, UK
brooklandsbooks.com

ISBN: 9781855204348   Part No. 545111/73   Ref: T169HH   2303/6W5

OFFICIAL TECHNICAL BOOKS

Brooklands Technical Books has been formed to supply owners, restorers and professional repairers with official factory literature.

Workshop Manuals

TR2 & TR3	502602	9780948207693
TR4 & TR4A	510322	9780948207952
TR5, TR250 & TR6 (Glove Box Autobooks Man.)		9781855201835
TR5-PI Supplement	545053	9781869826024
TR250 Supplement	545047	9781783181759
TR6 inc. TC & PI	545277/E2	9781869826130
TR7	AKM3079B	9781855202726
TR7	Autobooks Manual	9781783181506
TR8	AKM3981A	9781783180615
TR8	AKM 3971 and AKM 5015	9781783182053
Spitfire Mk 1, 2 & 3 & Herald 1200, 12/50, 13/60 & Vitesse 6	511243	9780946489992
Herald 948, 1200, 12/50, 13/60	Autobooks Man.	9781783181513
Spitfire Mk 4	545254H	9781869826758
Spitfire 1500	AKM4329	9781869826666
Spitfire Mk 3, 4, 1500 (Glove Box Autobooks Man.)		9781855201248
2000 & 2500	AKM3974	9781869826086
GT6 Mk 1, 2, 3 & Vitesse 2 Litre	512947	9780907073901
GT6 Mk 2, GT6+ & Mk 3 & Vitesse 2 Litre - Mk 2 1969-1973	Autobooks Manual	9781783181322
Stag	AKM3966	9781855200135
Stag	Autobooks Manual	9781783181490
Dolomite Sprint	AKM3629	9781855202825

Parts Catalogues

TR2 & TR3	501653	9780907073994
TR4	510978	9780907073949
TR4A	514837	9780907073956
TR5 PI	516915	9781783182060
TR250 US	516914	9781869826819
TR6 Sports Car 1969-1973	517785A	9780948207426
TR6 1974-1976	RTC9093A	9780907073932
TR7 1975-1978	RTC9814CA	9781855207943
TR7 1979+	RTC9828CC	9781870642231
TR7 & TR8	RTC9020B	9781870642651
Herald 13/60	517056	9781869826154
Vitesse 2 Litre Mk 2	517786	9781869826147
Stag	519579	9781870642996
GT6 Mk 1 and Mk 2 /GT6+	515754/2	9781783180448
GT6 Mk 3	520949/A	9780948207938
Spitfire Mk 3	516282	9781870642873
Spitfire Mk 4 & Spitfire 1500 1973-1974	RTC 9008A	9781869826659
Spitfire 1500 1975-1980	RTC9819CB	9781870642187
Dolomite Range 1976 on	RTC9822CB	9781855202764

www.brooklandsbooks.com

Owners Handbooks and Instruction Books

TR2 Instruction Book	501528/1	9781783181988
TR3 Instruction Book	501528/1	9781783181971
Triumph Competition Preparation Manual		
TR250, TR5 and TR6		9781783180011
Triumph Competition Preparation Manual		
TR250, TR5 and TR6 (2nd Ed.)		9781783182039
TR4	510326	9780948207662
TR4A	512916	9780948207679
TR4 and TR4A Competition Preparation Manual		9781783182022
TR5 PI	545034/2	9781855208544
TR250 (US)	545033	9780948207273
TR6	545078/1	9780948207402
TR6-PI	545078/2	9781855201750
TR6 (US 73)	545111/73	9781855204348
TR6 (US 75)	545111/75	9780948207150
TR7	AKM4332	9781870642736
TR8 (US)	AKM4779	9781855202832
Stag	545105	9781855206830
Spitfire Mk 3	545017	9780948207181
Spitfire Mk 4	545220	9781870642439
Spitfire Mk 4 (US)	545189	9781855207967
Spitfire 1500	RTC9221	9781870642453
Spitfire Competition Preparation Manual		9781870642606
GT6	512944	9781855201583
GT6 Mk 2 & GT6+	545057	9781855201422
GT6 Mk 3	545186	9780946489848
GT6, GT6+ & 2000 Competition Preparation Manual		9781855200678
2000, 2500 TC and 2500S	AKM3617/2	9781855202788
Herald 1200 12/50	512893/6	9781855200616
Herald 13/60	545037	9781855201415
Vitesse 2 Litre	545006	9781855200746
Vitesse Mk 2	545070/2	9781855200418
Vitesse 6	511236/5	9781855207974

Carburetters

SU Carburetters Tuning Tips & Technique	9781855202559
Solex Carburetters Tuning Tips & Techniques	9781855209770
Weber Carburettors Tuning Tips and Techniques	9781855207592

Truimph - Road Test Books

Triumph Herald 1959-1971	9781855200517
Triumph Vitesse 1962-1971	9781855200500
Triumph 2000 / 2.5 / 2500 1963-1977	9780946489237
Triumph GT6 Gold Portfolio 1966-1974	9781855202443
Triumph Spitfire Road Test Portfolio	9781855209534
Triumph Stag Road Test Portfolio	9781855208933
Triumph TR2 - TR3 1952-1960	9781870642583
Triumph TR2 & TR3 Gold Portfolio 1952-1961	9781855202429
Triumph TR4 - TR5 - TR250 1961-1968	9780948207532
Triumph TR6 Road Test Portfolio	9781855209268
Triumph TR7 & TR8 1975-1982	9781870642002
Triumph TR7 & TR8 Gold Portfolio 1975-1986	9781855202245
Road & Track on Triumph 1953-1967	9780946489473
Road & Track on Triumph 1967-1974	9780946489480
Road & Track on Triumph 1974-1982	9780946489282

Printed in Dunstable, United Kingdom